No Laughing Matter

by

David A. Quam

ISBN 978-1-64299-390-5 (paperback)
ISBN 978-1-64299-391-2 (digital)

Christian Faith Publishing, Inc.
832 Park Avenue
Meadville, PA 16335
www.christianfaithpublishing.com

Printed in the United States of America

This book is dedicated to my family:
To my wonderful wife, Carol, and to our four children:
Jesse David, Sarah Louise, Naomi Maria, and Lydia Pauline

CONTENTS

INTRODUCTION

Never Expect Gratitude

It was the middle of March in a Midwestern town. A young girl, age seven, was ice-skating on the lake. Suddenly, the ice broke and the girl fell through. She was slowly perishing. A young man, who was passing by, jumped in the water and rescued her. He called 911; and the emergency crew, the fire department, and the police all came. They slowly nursed the girl back to life. After they all were through doing their job, they returned to their respective stations.

Meanwhile, the young girl's mother arrived and the *young man had disappeared*. She heard about what had happened.

"Where was that young man?" she thought. The young man had entered the hospital and hung between life and death for weeks. He was suffering from pneumonia caused by the icy water. *He lost fifty pounds*. The mother continued to search for him. Finally, after several weeks, she found his address. She knocked on the door. He answered and said, "May I help you?"

She said, "Are you the man who pulled my daughter from the lake last March?"

He responded, "Yes, I am."

Then she asked, "All right, young man, where are her mittens?"

I tell that story every Thanksgiving to illustrate "*Never expect gratitude!*" Most people are temporarily shocked, and then they laugh. Some people say, "What an ungrateful mother!"

My point is that the story has a few elements of humor—a personal story, a buildup, and a punch line. We love to laugh. Laughing is good for us.

"Anatomy of a Laugh" from the book *The Happy Hunters*:

> Your whole body gets a kick out of a good chuckle.
>
> Here's what happens when you laugh, according to research.
>
> Your heart beats faster and your blood pressure rises temporarily.
>
> You breathe deeper and oxygenate more blood.
>
> Your body releases endorphins, your own natural pain killers, and you produce more immune cells.
>
> You burn seventy-eight times as many calories as you would in a resting state.
>
> Your diaphragm, facial muscles and internal organs all get bounced around in a message sometimes called "internal jogging."

"A merry heart doeth good like a medicine: but a broken spirit drieth the bones." (Proverbs 17:22)

The New English Bible translation of that verse says that "a merry heart makes a cheerful countenance, but low spirits sap a man's strength."

Why This Book Was Written

Two elements:

1. Pseudobulbar affect (PBA). What is Pseudobulbar affect? It is a medical condition that causes outbursts of uncontrolled or exaggerated emotion (either crying or laughing). I suffered a stroke on January 16, 2007, at 8:00 p.m., so I know how Pseudobulbar Affect feels. I forgot my name and I couldn't talk after my stroke. I never cried *too* much in my life before my stroke, but *after* my stroke, I experienced uncontrollable crying and laughing, sometimes at inappropriate times!
2. I memorized jokes, and I told them over and over in order to practice my speaking. Each time I tell the jokes, it got better and better. (My speaking got better. Not the jokes!)

So I decided to write a third book to follow: "*Wipeout: Journey of a Stroke Overcomer*" and "*Interrupted by God.*" My third book is entitled "*No Laughing Matter.*"

CHAPTER ONE

The Essence of Humor

Someone has said, "Comedy is the most powerful art form known to man." And yet it's somewhat complex. Why do we laugh? We need to laugh and weep to express our emotions. Someone else said, "Dying is easy, comedy is hard."

Dolphins play and so do otters. Whales communicate and take care of one another. Even geese do the same. But animals, fish, birds, reptiles, etc., don't laugh. They don't have the capacity to laugh.

But on the other hand, humans laugh. They need to laugh (and cry) to express their emotions. It was God's plan. Endorphins are hormones found mainly in the brain. Scientists say that endorphins are released by eating hot peppers and running long distances. Laughter makes us feel better! (And to run long distances while eating hot peppers! Forget it!)

Babies and toddlers laugh about forty times a day. Adults laugh about four times a day. Babies even smile before birth!

I enjoy listening to good comedians who are prepaid to be funny. I enjoy them no matter what their color is or their gender. If they are funny, I will laugh. No matter what their social class is or what country they are from, if they succeed in making me laugh, they have accomplished their purpose.

Some people are humorless. This is called frontal temporal dementia (FTD). They are totally lacking a sense of irony!

Some people fear being laughed at. This is called gelotophobia. There are some people who enjoy laughing at others to excess. They have katagelasticism.

Often the raw material of humor is tragic events. Humor is "tragedy plus time"—e.g., "Other than that, how was the play, Mrs. Lincoln?"

One of the most famous arias (songs) from the opera *I Pagliacci* is "Vesti La Guiba" (On with the Motly). Canio is the tenor. And Canio sings a song. He just found out that his wife has been cheating on him. In the opera, he plays a clown, but his heart is breaking because of the unfaithfulness of his wife.

Who said it? "If I don't experience laughter in heaven, I don't want to go there."

Will Rogers? No, Martin Luther said it!

I was a pastor for thirty-five years. I used humor in my preaching. A good, funny, clean joke can illustrate a point. Humor can open the window and let the fresh air come in.

Two men formed a partnership painting houses. They were prosperous in their new venture. One week they painted a little old lady's house. (It was huge.) Before they started painting, one of the men decided to "thin down the paint" in order to make the paint last longer! The other man didn't agree with his partner. When Friday came, they enjoyed the weekend. On Monday, the painter who had decided to "thin down the paint" told his partner, "I had a dream last night. In the dream, an angel spoke to me and said, 'Repaint, you thinner!'" (Repent, you sinner.)

I remember my mother telling about after her son, Kenny's death in Rochester, MN, at the Mayo Clinic. She took a bus home to Hawley, MN. It was a 350-mile trip. (I was two years old in 1944.) She could not understand the fact that people were laughing (going about their daily life), while she was grieving over her sixteen-year-old son's death!

I remember getting *MAD Magazine* when I was a kid. It had "Mommy, Mommy" jokes and "Shut Up" jokes.

Good humor needs a setting.

1. As a kid, I went to Sunday school every Sunday of my life—fifty-two weeks of the year. My father thought playing cards was a sin. "Mommy, Mommy, why don't I attend Sunday school like the rest of my class?" Mother's reply: "Shut up and deal!"
2. My father believed the Ten Commandments. (Thou shalt not kill.) "Mommy, Mommy, why is Daddy running down the road?" Mother's reply: "Shut up and reload!"

    The two preceding jokes are funny to me because of my background!

During the fifties, TV sitcoms (situation comedies) emerged. They were an offshoot of radio shows. All kinds of sitcoms were produced: *Jack Benny, The Great Gildersleeve, Life of Riley, The Show of Shows, I Love Lucy, Milton Berle*, etc.

They were usually half-hour shows. Then the sixties arrived with Andy Griffith. In the seventies: *MASH*, Mary Tyler Moore, and Carol Burnett. In the eighties there was Seinfeld, and in the nineties and throughout the twenty-first century there were many more.

The sitcoms are still on TV via reruns today. They were well-written and long-lasting. I still watch *Andy Griffith* reruns. I have watched some of the reruns numerous times, and I still never tire of watching them. They are timeless humor and clean humor in a setting of sometimes small-town America. All kinds of late-night shows have been on TV over the years: Steve Allen, Jack Parr, Johnny Carson, Jay Leno, David Letterman, Jimmy Kimmel, Stephen Colbert, Jimmy Fallon, etc.

I think Jesus laughed. He trained the twelve apostles for three years. Did the twelve have inside jokes? I like to think that they did.

I think a sense of humor is hereditary. For instance, my mother could imitate some of the individuals in our small town. She could do a perfect imitation of Rev. Haugi, who was a pastor for fifty-four years in Hawley, MN. She could also imitate Mrs. Furby telling about her ability to make homemade bread. When mother did these imitations, you would swear that Rev. Haugi and Mrs. Furby were sitting right next to you!

Our son Jesse could also do imitations. When we lived in Lincoln, NE, I was the pastor of Central Alliance Church for seven and a half years. After the Sunday evening service, we would have family time at home and Jesse would entertain us by imitating the choir director and some of the guest speakers. I do not know how my mother and our son Jesse could do these imitations so perfectly, but they could!

> Humor is anything that makes us laugh or smile.
> *What about dirty jokes?* (Sexual innuendo, double entedre, risqué.)
> A *clean* joke with double meaning: My wife had a bout with the Egyptian flu; she was about to be a mummy.

Have you ever heard of a clean traveling salesman joke? Hardly. There is plenty of clean humor instead of telling traveling salesman jokes, back-of-the-school-bus jokes, and men's and women's locker room jokes.

> "Let no corrupt words proceed out of your mouth." (Ephesians 4:29)
> "Neither filthiness nor foolish words or course jesting." (Ephesians 5:4)

Steve Allen said that no comedian ever makes up his own jokes. They are all recycled. Thanks to Vaudeville, and years before that, we have recycled jokes. I have plenty of joke books. They are all *recycled jokes.*

There are animal jokes, bar jokes, church jokes, ethnic jokes, traveling salesmen jokes, sports jokes, Thanksgiving jokes, military jokes, computer jokes, dog jokes, cat jokes, kids jokes, fat jokes, travel jokes, weather jokes, St. Peter jokes, old people jokes, knock-

knock jokes, and lawyer jokes. The list goes on and on and on. We all love to laugh.

Humor heals. In his book, *The Anatomy of an Illness*, Norman Cousins claims he was healed of a rare collagen disease by laughing! He watched old episodes of the *Three Stooges*, *Laurel and Hardy*, and other comedies.

CHAPTER TWO

I Learned to Speak All Over Again

I had a stroke (brain attack) on January 16, 2007, at 8:00 p.m. in Langford, SD.

Reprinted from my first book: *Wipeout: Journey of a Stroke Overcomer*:

> "I could see the skyline of Fargo-Moorhead. I had traveled that 20 miles from Hawley, MN, to Fargo, ND, hundreds of time by car, truck, bus, and train. But I had never traveled to Fargo by air in a helicopter. I got an unscheduled trip from Britton, SD, to Fargo, ND, on January 16, 2007. I had experienced a stroke. It was located in the left hemisphere of the brain which affected the area that controls the spoken word and written language. There were three of us in the helicopter. I was conscious and aware of them talking. What has happening to me?"

I spent twelve days in the Merit Care Hospital learning to function. I forgot my name. I tried to speak and could *not* speak.

I temporarily lost my memory. *But I could sing!* Our daughter, Naomi, visited with her one-year-old son, Jacob, and she asked me if it was okay for her to sing. I nodded my head yes. She started to sing the song "Great Is Thy Faithfulness" and I sang *with* her! But I still could not speak. Just six months earlier, I had performed in a melodrama at a small theater in South Dakota, finished a new sermon series at the church where I served as Pastor, and through diet and exercise shed 35 pounds. Then the stroke occurred. Each of my children came to visit at different times to help me and to encourage my wife, Carol. Lydia was the first to arrive. She had such a positive attitude and was so helpful! Naomi was the one who started to sing, and right after that I realized I could sing! Sarah came next and was there when I could, with assistance, walk down the hall. Later, Jesse drove all the way from Boston, Massachusetts, and visited and supported me when I was out of the hospital.

David performing in a melodrama in South Dakota six months before the stroke occurred

*David in MeritCare hospital a few days after
the stroke occurred in January, 2007*

Daughter Lydia Meyer with David in his room

***Jesse, David, and Carol with David's nephew, Jeff Quam
(after the stroke when we stayed in Moorhead)***

The stroke left me "wiped out." I had to relearn many things. Because I had temporarily lost my memory, *I slowly memorized jokes in order to learn how to talk all over again.*

Here is a list of some of my jokes:

My brother was named after my father. We called him "Dad."

When I was born, I was so homely that the doctor slapped my mother.

I got kicked out of a restaurant last evening because I forgot to wear a tie. So I rummaged through my car and found a set of jumper cables and wrapped it around my neck like a neck tie. When I entered the restaurant again, the waiter said to me, "Okay, you can eat, but don't start anything!"

I am doing a scientific experiment: crossing bees with fireflies—to make honey at night.

My wife and I purchased a waterbed, but we began to drift apart. I put my money underneath my waterbed. When the waterbed got a leak in it, I liquidated my assets.

I heard about a woman who was married four times. Once to a banker, once to a stage director, once to a clergyman, and once to a funeral director. One for the money, two for the show, three to get ready, and four to go.

I met a couple. She was a snake charmer and he was a funeral director. Their bathroom towels were monogrammed with the words: "Hiss" and "Hearse."

I just heard on the radio that Snap, Crackle, and Pop were murdered. The police suspect a cereal (serial) killer.

I once heard about a man who was blown up by a dynamite explosion. On his tombstone were these words: "Rest in Pieces."

Winston Churchill and Lady Astor did *not* get along. One day, Lady Astor remarked to Churchill: "Sir, if you were my husband, I would put arsenic in your tea." Winston Churchill replied, "Madame, if you were my wife, I would drink it!"

Through researching our family tree, I found out that my great-great-great-great-great aunt was at the Boston Tea Party. She was the last "old bag" thrown overboard.

Last night, I dreamed I was a muffler. When I woke up this morning, I was exhausted.

I visited a prisoner the other day. He was *sewing*. I asked him, "Are you *sowing*?" He answered: "No, I am reaping."

My name is Cliff: drop over some time.

Last night I dreamed I swallowed a giant marshmallow. When I woke up this morning, my pillow was missing.

Where do guns go to be baptized? "Winchester Cathedral."

I heard about a man who stayed up all night to find out what happens when the sun goes down in the west. And in the morning, it finally dawned on him.

A husband forgot his wife's birthday. She was livid (angry). She said, "Tomorrow I want to rise at 6:00 a.m. and find a present out in the driveway that goes from zero to two hundred in two seconds." She went to bed. At 6:00 a.m., she stepped outside and found a small package in the driveway. It contained a bathroom scale.

Three actors were discussing roles. They decided to portray composers' lives. Tom Hanks said, "I'll be Beethoven." Tom Cruise said, "I'll be Mozart." Arnold Schwarzenegger said: "I'll be Back" (Bach).

What is the definition of mixed emotions? Seeing your mother-in-law drive over a cliff in your brand-new car.

I once had a cross-eyed teacher who couldn't keep her pupils straight.

If a midwife has a problem with delivering a baby is that called a "midwife crises"?

I am three-fourths Norwegian. How did the Norwegian get eighty-eight holes in his face? By trying to learn how to eat with a fork.

I had to quit the ministry because of illness. My congregation got sick of me!

One day it happened: George got engaged to Sue Ann. "Let's have a big wedding" said George.

"Oh, that is wonderful," replied Sue Ann.

"Let's have a horse-drawn carriage to drive us to our honeymoon destination," said George.

"Fantastic," said Sue Ann. So it happened. George married Sue Ann in a big wedding. As George planned, they had a horse-drawn carriage. A mile down the road, the horse balked. "That's one," said George. Another mile down the road, the horse balked once more. "That's two," said George. Another mile down the road, the horse balked the third time. "That's three," said George. George got out of the carriage and hit the horse with a sledgehammer and knocked the horse out cold. Sue Ann was horrified! She said, "George, have you lost your mind?"

George replied, "That's one!"

This is a true story: In Lincoln, NE, I served as a pastor of the Central Alliance Church for seven and a half years. During that time, I sang for many funerals. At one particular funeral, I sang for a man who was cremated. His last name was "Chestnut." In the forenoon, I was on the phone getting the words to the song "Danny Boy" from my sister. Finally, I got the words written down. While I was waiting to sing, I thought, "This man is Mr. Chestnut and he was cremated. Why not sing 'Chestnut Roasting on an Open Fire?'" I sang "Danny Boy" instead.

An actor looked exactly like Abe Lincoln. He was tall, had a mole on his face and walked with a characteristic gait. One day he read in the *Variety News* that a playwright had written a new play about Abe Lincoln. The actor was excited. He went home and shined up his mole and wore his top hat and walked up and down the street, waiting to be discovered. He finally found the playwright's home and knocked on the door. The butler opened the door and said, "May I help you?"

The actor replied, "Here I am."

The butler asked, "What do you mean?"

The actor said: "Destiny has called me to be the star of the play about Abe Lincoln."

The butler said: "I am sorry, but the part has been filled by another actor."

However, *not* all was lost: on the way home, the actor was assassinated!

A bunch of morons were starting a choir. They could only sing while drinking Tab pop (a Coca-Cola product) and eating apples. They called themselves "The Moron Tab and Apple Choir."

Orville and Wilbur were Wright (right).

A cat ate two robins who were basking in the sun. The cat said, "I just love Baskin-Robins!"

A termite walks into a bar and says, "Is the bar-tinder (bar-tender) here?"

A skeleton walks into a bar and orders a drink and a mop.

The scene was a waiting room for expectant fathers. A nurse was reporting to them the circumstance concerning the births of their children. The first father worked for Doublemint Gum and the nurse told him he had twins. The second expectant father worked for 3M Company and the nurse told him he had triplets. The third expectant father worked for 7 Up Company and the nurse told him he had septuplets. The last expectant father passed out in the corner of the room. He worked for Phillips 66.

A pastor I know performed the marriage ceremony for a young couple at the parsonage. After the ceremony was over, the pastor congratulated the new husband. The groom asked the pastor, "How much do I owe you for performing the marriage ceremony for us?"

The pastor answered, "I tell you what, why don't you pay me according to how good looking your bride is?" The groom thought for a moment and pulled out a quarter and gave it to the pastor. The pastor was curious, so he lifted up the new bride's veil to take a look at her. Then he said to the groom: "Just a minute, I'll get your change."

A guy in New York desperately wanted to see a Broadway musical show. He thought, "How can I get a ticket?" He searched for two months and finally got a ticket for a matinee performance. He rented a tuxedo and the day arrived. He enjoyed the first act and after the applause died down, he noticed an empty seat beside him. He struck up a conversation with the little old lady who sat next to the empty seat. He said, "I can't understand. It took me two months to get my ticket to this show. And to my surprise someone had a ticket and failed to use it."

She replied, "That seat belonged to my husband. He died."

"Oh, I'm so sorry," the man said. After a pause, he asked her, "Couldn't you have given the ticket to a relative or a friend or a neighbor?"

"No," she said, "they are all at his funeral."

CHAPTER THREE

What Makes David Laugh?

My father owned a junkyard and fur-buying business. In the spring and summer, I would find myself loading scrap iron, selling parts, and doing all sorts of things related to the scrap-iron and metal business. In the fall and winter seasons, I worked with fur-bearing animals like raccoon, mink, muskrat, beaver, weasel, etc.

The following is an excerpt from an article by my brother *Butch* about how he skinned his way through college:

> My father was a wild fur buyer in the small Northwestern Minnesota community of Hawley, MN. He bought the furry creatures from farmers and trappers. They would bring them to my dad's place of business and he would travel several counties buying from those trappers and hunters he knew had fur to sell. The animals were then processed and shipped to New York where a fur broker would sell the skins to manufacturers in European countries, as well as America and Canada. My dad's New York fur broker often told

him that the raccoon found in the Cormorant Lake area were among the highest quality in the world. I began my "fur career" in 1946 at age 6. I began skinning muskrats at 12 under the tutelage of my Uncle Louie. Skinning other animals soon followed—raccoon, mink, weasel, beaver, fox, rabbit, badger, wolf, timber wolf, lynx, bobcat, otter, opossum—even dead sheep. There was also the process of scraping and stretching the skins on either a wire or board stretcher.

Butch working with a beaver pelt he had skinned

I would work for my dad on weekends, holidays, and during the summers in his scrap metal business. I earned enough money to pay for my books, tuition, rent, food, travel, and date money. The travel from school was 250 miles one way on the Northern Pacific Mainsteamer, Greyhound Bus, or hitchhiking. One time when I was on the train and had just wrapped some 25 cuts with tape, I decided to have a hamburger in the dining car.

As I sat down, a lady saw my hands and asked, "What happened to you?" I calmly answered, "I'm studying surgery and I'm not very good at it."

When I was a Junior in High School, my dad bought 75 skunks from a trapper. I volunteered to process them, starting at midnight on a Monday. I worked from 7:30 in the morning, skinning, scraping the fat off the skins, and stretching them on the wire stretchers. I walked 3 blocks to our home and undressed in the entry way. My mom burned my clothes in the garbage barrel. I took two baths, got dressed and went to school. I walked into Mrs. Berg's geometry class and sat down by Marlene Olson. She turned to me and said, "I smell a skunk." I sniffed the air and replied, "I do too. There must be a skunk nearby." My dad bought timber wolves from some of the airplane hunters in Northern Minnesota. They were difficult to skin—very hidebound. I skinned one that weighed 125 pounds. It took me two hours to skin the huge wolf. My dad had the wolf tanned.

That next summer, I attended school at the University of Minnesota. I decided to have some fun with the wolf skin. I would wrap it around me, tying the leg skins in front of me, and draping the head skin over my head. I would wait for the students to walk on the sidewalk at 2:00 a.m. in front of where I lived. I would then run out on the porch howling and scaring the wits out of the poor, unsuspecting students from India, Africa, and Asia. The girls especially got freaked out. My howl was very realistic.

I could write a book on all the interesting and sometimes gross experiences I have encoun-

tered. I may write that book and have even for-
mulated alternative titles: How about, "The
Grossest Job in the World" or "Making Money
With a Knife" or "Hey Lady—Let Me Tell You
How Your Fur Coat Started."

As I look back, I was very fortunate to have
had this opportunity to work at processing the
furry creatures. It provided for my education and
taught me to work hard. (Butch)

Many men would work for my dad. He was a good business-
man, and he was honest. Dad would not allow dirty jokes in our
home. But he could not control the speech of his hired help. I myself
heard many dirty stories and poems from the men who worked for
my dad, especially the servicemen.

Andrew L. Quam and his family in a
picture taken 100 years ago

My dad (born in 1897) had thirteen brothers and sisters. He had
three brothers who died alcoholics. One of his brothers was named
Louis. He was short, superstitious, and loved to drink. He was bitter. He

served in WWII. His job was burying dead bodies. Dead bodies smell. He never married. He was known as Uncle Louie. He was the topic of all our family gatherings. No matter what we talked about, we would end up talking about Uncle Louie. One time, Uncle Louie was drunk and bothering my mother. Aunt Lila, Uncle Louie's tall, stern sister, grabbed him by his ear and marched him downtown and into the local hotel.

On Saturday, during the winter, we were all busy skinning and scraping animals. My brother Butch skinned and scraped raccoon. I skinned fox. My two nephews, Byron and Jeff, skinned muskrats. My older brother, Lawrence, skinned mink. My Uncle Louie skinned rabbits. My brother Butch would hang a car radio from the ceiling of the skinning house, so we could listen to the Metropolitan Opera Broadcast at 1:00 p.m. on Saturday. (Uncle Louie would *not* appreciate the opera.) About 3:00 p.m., Louie could not control his desire for an alcoholic beverage. In anticipation of drinking on a Saturday night, he could not stand to listen to the Mozart sextet sung in German or Italian any longer and he got angry and blew up. (What Louie said I will not print.)

One time at a dance, my father was going to let either Morrell or Louie use his car to take a girl home. At 4:00 a.m., a fight broke out between Morrell and Louie. A sheep shearer, Clarence Jarandson, broke up the fight and got mad and dumped the old slop barrel on top of Uncle Morrell and Uncle Louie. I don't know which Uncle took the girl home. I think neither of them did because they both smelled so bad from the alcohol and slop barrel.

Uncle Louie would go through cars, one junk car after another. One time, I was in the car driving with him and he announced to me that he had no brakes. He would drive slowly. When he arrived at a STOP sign, he would turn the car motor off. (Scary!)

One time he was driving and he turned a corner and fell out of the car! The car kept moving and hit a tree. (My friend Greg Anderson saw Louie do this.)

Uncle Louie was a good fighter until he lost a Saturday evening brawl to a big guy in some tavern. I picked him up after the brawl was over. His head was twice the normal size.

Louie was the thirteenth member of the Quam clan. He was superstitious. My dad offered him $13.00 for a mink that Louie had trapped. Louie would only accept $12.50.

Louie died at age seventy-four of lung cancer. (He rolled his own cigarettes and used Prince Albert tobacco.) He died in a hospital in Fargo, ND. He died a very bitter man. Louie is buried in Hawley, MN. So sad.

Central City Opera Company: The following is a memoir I wrote for a Valentine's Day contest that the National Public Radio station in Minnesota held around the year 2002.

My wife, Carol Asborno, and I met in the summer of 1966. We were two of twenty-eight singers who successfully auditioned for the opera chorus at the Central City Opera Company in Central City, CO. This included singing in nine major opera performances a week plus smaller bit parts, opera workshops, and opera training. That summer, the operas were *Carmen, The Italian Girl in Algiers*, and *The Ballad of Baby Doe*. By the summer's end Carol and I had fallen in love. We spent the following academic year teaching. I taught in Battle Lake, MN, and she taught near Denver, CO, in the town of Lakewood. During that year, we kept the US Postal Service and the Alexander Graham Bell phone company in business with our frequent correspondence.

*David in his costume from the opera, **The Merry Widow**, performed in Central City, CO, in 1967.*

The following spring I successfully auditioned for the opera company again. I was the only one of the twenty-eight that retuned (this broke tradition, but I was glad for obvious reasons). That was the summer of 1967, and we performed *The Merry Widow, Don Pasquale,* and *The Masked Ball.* Carol taught that summer forty miles down the highway in Lakewood, CO. As the summer progressed, I began to think that this relationship should become a duet. I ordered a ring from our jeweler back in my hometown of Hawley, MN. (Earlier I had "stolen" a ring from Carol to get the correct size.) I then thought to myself that the waltz the on-stage sextet played in the last murderous act of *The Masked Ball* would be very fitting for the time when I would propose to Carol. I thought, why not have them play it live at the Episcopal shrine up on the hill from the opera house, which was eight thousand feet above sea level? Again I thought to myself, let's do it.

The ring arrived in the mail. I then planned the logistics for the evening of July 18, 1967, with two friends and fellow singer, David

Hall and Patrick Robinson. We built a throne, put candles on either side of it, and got twelve red roses and a pillow to kneel on. I then arranged for my two friends to drive the six musicians, members of the Denver Symphony, and their delicate and expensive instruments up the hill to the shrine. Now all that was left was to ask the sextet to play. I can't remember having to call upon more courage than I did the night I asked them to play for the special event I was planning—that of asking Carol to marry me. The evening of inquiry arrived. We were performing the same opera, *The Masked Ball*, and were between acts. The sextet was sitting together in costume off stage. All seven of us were soon to be on-stage for the last act of the opera. I approached them and introduced myself. After a few remarks stating that I was perfectly normal, I proposed my idea to them. There was silence. As I spoke, one of the musicians, a lady cellist, kept staring at me as she puffed away on her cigarillo. After what seemed to be an eternity, one of them stated that they would think about it. After a few days, they returned and told me they would do it.

Left to right: David Hall (tenor),
Patrick Robinson (baritone) and David

Finally, Saturday night arrived. The Verdi operas always lasted a long time. After the opera, around 11:30 p.m., I showered, and grabbed my car. I picked up Carol and drove her to the site, taking a different route than my two friends and the six musicians had taken. As we arrived, I asked Carol to close her eyes. When I opened the car door, the music could be heard carrying beautifully through the mountain air. It was midnight, and it had just rained. When we reached the throne, the music had ended and the sextet had left. It was now silent except for the midnight sounds of the town below. I then asked her to open her eyes. I placed the ring on her finger, gave her the roses, and knelt on one knee on the pillow. I asked Carol to marry me. She said, "Yes!" I then took my Bible and read her favorite

Psalm, chapter 91. The flickering candles made it tough to read. We then left the site. We drove back down the mountain to the town. Carol drove her MG back to Denver, and I went back to my room.

Carol & David after the opera performance

The sextet plays a selection from "The Masked Ball" before the proposal

After the proposal (1:00 AM)

At the party, the day after proposal

The next day, the opera chorus served cake and pop to the entire company outside the opera house after the afternoon performance. I blew my whole paycheck that week for the musicians and the reception (I gave the chorus money to make the cakes). The ring took more than one paycheck!

Later that summer, we both signed contracts to teach in Barnesville, MN, for the following year. We got married on December 27, 1967, in my home church in Hawley, MN, where we both then attended. It was twenty degrees below zero that night. Six of my nephews buried my car in snow after the wedding and wore down the battery trying to drive it out of the snow.

We spend most of our honeymoon in St. Paul, MN. We watched the Ice Bowl on TV (Green Bay versus Dallas) instead of going to church that Sunday, for it was thirty degrees below zero! Our car battery froze solid. When we got home, I bought a new battery.

In 1972, I went into the ministry and later entered seminary and became a pastor. Carol and I together raised our four children. We have pictures of that wonderful 1967 summer event when I proposed to Carol. Of course, the marriage did not end in murder as the opera did! We have a great life together and are still in love.

Postscript: the sextet bought us a bottle of champagne after I paid them. Neither of us drink, so one year later, Carol and I shook up the big bottle and let it blast out all over my mother's garden.

During our stay in Central City, we traveled looking for a church in a nearby town. That church didn't believe in instrumental music "organ, piano, guitars, drums, etc." We sat in the balcony while the congregation sat near the front. All I can remember is that the congregation sang a capella. There were thirteen in the congregation. Have you ever listened to thirteen monotones sing? We did. We looked for another church.

During my *first* year singing in Central City, Carol and I were two of the twenty-eight singers in the chorus of the opera. During a performance, there was something that happened that I still laugh about. We were performing the opera *Carmen*. The tenor, Thomas Hayward, who sang the role of Don Jose, was an understudy for another singer who fell ill earlier that year. Tommy had trouble memorizing his lines, so he relied heavily on help from the other members of the opera cast. During the first act, he just lost it! He blurted out, "She's been wounded!" *Wrong.* The whole cast broke out in laughter. The only thing that prevented the curtain from coming down was Carmen singing and laughing in character. I laughed for three days. I never forgot the look on Thomas Hayward's face. I still laugh fifty years later.

Speaking of Opera

I remember the spring of 1964. I was student teaching in the campus school of Moorhead State University. I was supervised by my old band teacher from Hawley, MN. At Hawley, he didn't get along with one janitor. (He thought he was lazy.) One of the student teaching lesson plans was a unit on opera. I presented a multiple choice test on opera including the names of other fictitious characters as the options. *I also included the name of the old, lazy janitor.* One of the questions on the opera test was "Name the lazy Italian composer who used to lay in bed and compose." "G. Rossini." One of the students' choice was the old lazy janitor. My brother and I laughed at this for days!

Tipping Outhouses Over

One Halloween night, we thought it was a good idea to tip outhouses over. We were successful. We laughed and laughed. We suddenly thought, "Who needs Halloween?" So two weeks later, we tipped over another outhouse. We tipped over outhouses every Friday night after the basketball games. We tipped over one of them three times. Finally we attempted to tip over a fourth time, but chains and ropes had been put into place. We gave up tipping over outhouses forever.

DAVID A. QUAM

The Off-Key Piano

About thirty-five years ago, we visited the steam threshers reunion in Rollag, MN, near Hawley, MN. They started this reunion in the 1950s. During the course of the events, it grew so large it became a village. There is even a railroad track that encircles it. The events included many kinds of workers, an all-you-can-eat breakfast, parades, antiques, schoolhouses, and much more. We visited one schoolhouse where the coordinator of it played the piano. She stopped to wait on a customer. I stepped to the piano and played a song but it was off-key (it was terrible). I saw her look out of the corner of her eye as she endured the awful sound.

Laughing in Church

What's more tempting than laughing in church? We all have experienced that. In church, especially a quiet dignified church service, it's almost overwhelming. I remember stuffing my handkerchief in my mouth to keep from laughing from the off-key singing in the old Methodist church.

The Bus Trip to Minneapolis

My brother Butch and I were on our way to the University of Minnesota by Greyhound Bus. We thought it would be fun to give the people riding the bus something to laugh at. Both of us were readers of *MAD Magazine*. One of us had just bought the recent issue. In this particular issue, there were several pages of lyrics to popular songs. The songs were poking fun at various people, institutions, occupations, etc. We decided to start singing them. Butch and I used to sing duets at churches and could harmonize fairly well. When we would finish a song, the small crowd on the Greyhound Bus would break out in applause. As the afternoon went on, the bus began to fill up. When we completed the pages of songs, we would start over. On the way home to MSU, I traveled on the Northern Pacific Main Steamer Train (about 250 miles). During the trip, I heard somebody talking to another gentleman. It seems like the traveler was on the same bus that Butch and I were on when we entertained the travelers with our songs.

Trip to White Earth Island

This happened in about 1960. There were six of us in our gang of teenage boys. We decided to take an adventurous trip to an island on White Earth Lake north of Detroit Lakes, Minnesota. In order to make the trip, we needed to have a vehicle that would carry all six of us and the camping gear for the two day adventure. The only possibility we could think of at the time was our pastor's Volkswagen bus, which was large enough to carry all six boys with the camping gear on the top. I still don't remember how, but we managed to talk Pastor Russ Crosby into letting us use it. I believe that Butch let him use his '54 Chevy for the two days. Russ told me one time that his father told him that he was a distant cousin of Bing Crosby. Whether or not it was true we do not know. However, Russ had a booming baritone voice. (Russ had thirteen children, who are all in the ministry, and he had sixty-five grandchildren and over one hundred great-grand-children). Butch, Russ Crosby, August Frisk, and I became a quartet who sang gospel music during the time Russ was the pastor of the Christian and Missionary Alliance Church in Hawley, MN (we also sang on KFGO Radio every week for two years).

We took off late on a Friday afternoon in July. I remember we had a quantity of fireworks in the top carrier. It is over an hour's drive from Hawley to White Earth Lake. My dad and brother Lawrence fished this lake quite often. Dad and Pastor Russ also fished the big lake. We arrived and needed to make two trips to the island with half the crew, the camping gear, and the food. It had been a beautiful day and promised to be a beautiful evening. The area we chose for our tents and bed rolls was a fairly clear piece of ground. We weren't sure, but we think there were some animals on the island. Our next chore was to start the grill and prepare hamburgers, hot dogs, beans, and roast marshmallows for s'mores. Some of the crew brought with them a choice piece of steak to pig out on.

We had a portable radio which blasted the top hits of the 1950s and 1960s. Butch would rather listen to Beethoven and Mozart, but he didn't want to risk a mutiny. It was ten o'clock when we hit the sack and maybe midnight before we were all quiet. The next morning, we were up at 7:00 a.m. I am not sure why we decided to chop down a good-sized tree, but we did. On Saturday, we hid our gear on the island and drove to Itasca State Park. There we saw where the mighty Mississippi River begins. From there we went shopping for some camping supplies and food on our way back to the island. The next day was Sunday, and Butch and I had promised some of our gang's parents that we would try to get them to church. I chose Park Rapids, Minnesota. Because it was a resort town, the church was packed. The only thing we could do was sit on the church lawn and listen to the service and the sermon through the windows. Next, we ate at a hamburger shop. Then it was time to head for home. Most of the crew slept on the way back. A good time was had by all.

New Year's Eve Mooring Stone

It is important to remember that controversy involving the mooring stone had its roots with a very few people of the Lutheran and Catholic churches. The two individuals were Leif Ericson (whom the Lutherans viewed as a hero when he supposedly was the first to come to America when he was in Minnesota around 1000 AD), and Christopher Columbus (whom the Catholics claim was the first person who really discovered America in 1492). Fast forward to the 1960s where the editors of two western Minnesota newspapers, who were actually good friends would get together and plan and scheme how they would publish news articles in their respective weekly newspapers. This news would create some hot controversy. This would consist of the sports with the two schools, the success of their fishermen, or any hot topic—the more controversial, the better. Mooring stones were being discovered near Hawley, MN, at this time. A mooring stone is a huge rock in which the Norwegian Vikings would drill a hole the size of a quarter in which a steel peg tied to a rope would be inserted into the rock and secure the Viking ship. The general theory reported by the editor to the Hawley people was that the Vikings were in the Hawley area around 10 AD. The opposition theory was that this theory was all hogwash.

Enter a group of college and high school kids (our gang) from Hawley who would create some type of debate to those observing from a distance. These kids (our gang) manufactured a mooring stone by using a scrapped Maytag washing machine. Using the clothes housing aluminum tub, tipping it upside down, filling it with cement, embedding a Viking snuff can in the fresh cement, placing a steel three-fourths inch hold into the cement seven-inch deep, then letting it set up for thirty-six hours. The aluminum mold was then broke off leaving the mooring stone.

It was New Year's Eve and time for some college boys (our gang) to have some fun. It was decided that the goal was to have the stone be exposed to as many of the approximately 1,500 Hawley residents as possible. Since the post office was going to be open on the next day, New Year's Day, on the sidewalk in front of the post office was the logical spot for it. Many people saw it when they came in for their mail. Most just laughed. Somehow the story got into the *Minneapolis Tribune*. Of course it got published in the *Hawley Herald* on the front page.

TV Wrestling

During our high school and college years, we would spend Saturday evening bowling in Moorhead, MN, then head out for Fargo, ND, across the border to attend TV Wrestling at 10:30 p.m. at WDAY channel 6. Our group made up half of the audience. We would sing and taunt the wrestlers. At 11:30 p.m., we went to eat pizza and go home. Sometimes we would stop and eat at the Glyndon Grill, which was located half way between Fargo-Moorhead and Hawley. Someone would say to me, "Dave, hit a high C." So I would stand up on a chair and hit a high note. Another time we accompanied my brother, Butch, on Highway 10 at midnight to sing for him as he entered the bus to go home to Minneapolis. Imagine the shock of the passengers who heard the quartet sing out, "You are my sunshine . . . my only sunshine . . ."

Most of our gang played instruments. We formed a small band called the Dudes. We would play at the local rodeo. Another time we challenged the local Legion players to a baseball game. (We played our horns between innings.) We would play in many local parades, and in downtown, Hawley during Friday night when the stores were open until 9:30 p.m.

Fishing in Hawley

In Hawley, MN, population 1,500 (counting the cats and dogs), there were two fishing organizations: The Fishing Syndicate and The Honest Rod-Benders. It was written up in the *Hawley Herald* newspaper every week. Minnesota, land of ten thousand lakes, is a wonderful place to live. During the summer the topic all around town was: "Where are they biting?" (A farmer, years ago, had twelve daughters. So they named twelve lakes after his twelve daughters: Lake Melissa, Lake Sally, Lake Lydia, Lake Lida, etc.) All kinds of fishing jokes were told over and over. (I caught a fish so big that the picture of it weighed thirty-five pounds.) (I caught a fish so big that I shingled my roof with its scales.)

Radio Time

Before TV came along, we used to gather around a radio for our listening enjoyment during the fifties. Such programs as *The Lone Ranger, Jack Benny, Mr. District Attorney, The Shadow, My Friend Irma*, etc.

A robber says to Jack Benny: "Your money or your life." A long pause . . . Jack Benny says, "I'm thinking, I'm thinking." Followed by two minutes of laughter.

David's Sister, Patty, Makes David Laugh

Two scenes (and many more) regarding David's younger sister, Patty, continue to make David laugh. She was eighth in the Quam clan, I was the seventh. My sister was somewhat spoiled but a good person. She was a good talker and schemer. One time she was using our father's car. Before using the car, our father would check the mileage and write it down. One time, Patty and a friend were in Ulen, MN, fourteen miles from our home in Hawley, MN. Suddenly she realized that she had exceeded the mileage that our father had written down. So she drove the car backwards all the way back to Hawley using gravel country roads. The car drove backwards for fourteen total miles.

Another time, Patty found herself disappointed in her blind date. So she told him to stop at a local restaurant so she could use the phone. She called a friend and arranged for him to pick her up on the backside of the restaurant. She proceeded to catch her new ride leaving her blind date behind.

There Will Never Be Another You

Years ago, I was teaching voice lessons at Crown College before I entered the ministry. We were eating lunch where I was relaying to the music faculty my paper I wrote on the results of the music played on the loudspeaker and subsequence effect on the workforce. They even played music in the barn. The results were fantastic. The cows produced more milk, the cats caught more mice, the pigs grew larger, the sheep grew more wool, and the horses grew stronger. The result of playing music in the barn was sensational. Except on the ram. He would butt his head on the side of the barn over and over again. Suddenly it occurred to the farmer that was playing the music that the selection was having a negative effect on the ram. The music they were playing was "There Will Never Be Another Ewe" (You). And now... the rest of the story: the above, 'my paper on the effects of music played for animals' was in fact, entirely fabricated.

CHAPTER FOUR

Communication and Imitation

Created for Community

One of the oldest and most cherished doctrines of historic Christian theology is the doctrine of the Trinity. The Nicene Creed (c. AD 325) summarizes the Trinity this way:

"I believe in one God, the Father Almighty, Maker of heaven and earth, and of all things visible and invisible. And in one Lord Jesus Christ, the only begotten Son of God, begotten of the Father before all worlds; God of God, Light of Light, very God of very God; begotten, not made, being of one substance with the Father . . . And I believe in the Holy Ghost, the Lord and Giver of Life; who proceeds from the Father and the Son; who with the Father and the Son together is worshipped and glorified."

Authors Robert H. Thune and Will Walker say the following in their book *The Gospel Centered Community*: The Trinity means that God himself is in a community. More accurately, God *is* community: one God, three persons. "Before all worlds (before any sort of human community existed) there was God, dwelling in perfect, loving harmony in his threefold being."

In the biblical account of creation, this Triune God says, "Let us make man in our image" (Genesis 1:26). Human beings are made to *image* God to reflect his likeness. That's why our longing for community is something we all want, if it's part of being made in God's image bearers. So if deep community is something we all want, if it's part of being made in God's image, then what makes it so hard to attain?

What keeps us from achieving the type of meaningful human relationships that God wired us for?

1. Sin: "All have sinned and come short of the glory of God" (Romans 3:23). We broke our fellowship with God by sin.
2. *We need each other.* The Greek word, Koinonia, means: "The fellowship of God and others by the power of the Holy Spirit."

Many "one anothers" are in the Bible; here are twelve examples of "one anothers."

Building Up One Another

Members of one another: "So we who are many, are one body in Christ, and individually members of one another" (Romans 12:5, NASB). No individual Christian can function effectively by himself. No member of Christ's body should feel he is more important than another member of Christ's body—Christians should work hard at maintaining unity in the body of Christ.

Devoted to one another: "Be devoted to one another in brotherly love" (Romans 12:10). The term "brotherly love" (Philadelphia) refers to the love that should exist between brothers and sisters within family units. The word brothers literally means "from the same womb."

Honor one another: "Honor one another above yourselves" (Romans 12:10). "Do nothing out of selfish ambition or vain conceit, but in humility consider others better than yourselves. Each of you should look not only to your own interests, but also to the interests of others" (Philippians 2:3–4).

Be of the same mind with one another: "Now may the God who gives perseverance and encouragement grant you to be the same mind with one another according to Christ Jesus" (Romans 15:5). Unity—not union—must be maintained. And within unity, there is diversity.

Accept one another: "Accept one another, then, just as Christ accepted you in order to bring praise to God" (Romans 15:7). Don't judge one another and don't show partiality. Instead, lovingly accept one another.

Admonish one another: "And concerning you, my brethren, I myself also am convinced that you yourselves are full of goodness, filled with all knowledge, and able to admonish one another" (Romans 15:14). The basis for being competent to admonish is "Being full of goodness" and "complete in knowledge"—i.e., a righteous person who has a complete knowledge of the Word is to admonish.

Greet one another (Romans 16:3–6, 16): We should greet all Christians warmly—perhaps with a "holy handshake."

Serve one another: "You, my brothers, were called to be free. But do not use your freedom to indulge the sinful nature; rather, serve one another in love" (Galatians 5:13). We are to experience true freedom by becoming slaves to God and slaves to one another by serving one another.

Bear one another's burdens: "Bear one another's burdens, and thus fulfill the law of Christ" (Galatians 6:2). Restoration of a wayward Christian must be done by spiritual Christians, usually by more than one person, with genuine humility, cautiously, and prayerfully.

Bearing with one another: "Be completely humble and gentle; be patient, bearing with one another in love" (Ephesians 4:2). We all need practice, a forgiving spirit and a commitment to work hard at "putting up with one another."

Submit to one another: "Submit to one another out of reverence for Christ" (Ephesians 5:21). We must have mutual submission:

toward one another. We need to yield to one another's admonition and advice. The more, "authority" we have, the more we must have a submissive heart (like Moses, Paul, and Jesus).

Encourage one another: "Therefore encourage one another and build each other up" (1 Thessalonians 5:11).

Imitation

"Be imitators of God, therefore, as dearly loved children and live a life of love, just as Christ loved us and gave Himself up for us as a fragrant offering and sacrifice to God." ((Ephesians 5:1–2)

My brother Butch and I grew up in an ideal neighborhood that was reminiscent of the movie *The Sandlot*. We would play softball and baseball together, and play run-sheep-run, red robin, touch football, and other activities.

But there was one thing that we did not do together: attend movies, which were then called "shows." I remember that often when Butch, our friends, and I would be doing all of these activities, someone would yell out, "There's a movie at the Garrick Theater!" The person would then mention movies such as *Tarzan* or *Ma and Pa Kettle* or *Roy Rogers*. Our friends would head off to the movies and Butch and I would go home, because our strict father would not allow us to attend movies. We were also forbidden from smoking, drinking, swearing, playing cards, playing pool, dancing, and working and playing ball on Sundays.

Therefore, I did not go to movies until I entered college. Finally, when I was nineteen years old, I attended a show. It was a documentary on Adolf Hitler shown in Fargo, ND. When I was about twenty years old, I went on a date and saw the cartoon *101 Dalmatians* in Detroit Lakes, MN.

In 1953, when television came to our area, my brother and I were mesmerized by it. We went over to the neighbor's house to watch it. Finally, in 1954, my father broke down and bought a television set from the local Thysell Brothers Department Store. The first complete show I watched was *Wild Bill Hickcock*. My father also had strict rules about the television

Invariably the television had variety shows, which had their origins in the old Vaudeville programs. These would feature comedians who would do all sorts of impersonations, none of which I found amusing because I didn't recognize the people they were imitating. I had missed watching movies for nineteen years.

I never forgot a certain scene on a television western where there was a close-up of a cowboy shooting a six-gun at the enemy. I recognized him right away. It was *James Cagney*. I had seen so many impersonations of him that I easily recognized him from the impersonations.

My experience with the television impersonations illustrated the following verse. "No one has ever seen God: but if we love one another, God lives in us and His love is made complete in us" (1 John 4:12, NIV). This verse aptly describes *Incarnational Living*.

About one hundred years ago, a Charlie Chaplin lookalike contest was held. All the fans of this classic silent movie star dressed up and tried to win the contest. The first and second place winners were announced. The third place winner was a surprise! Charlie Chaplin *himself* had entered the contest and won third place! Think of that! Two individuals were judged to look *more* like Charlie Chaplin than *he* did. This is quite a revelation. "No one has ever seen God: but if we love one another, <u>God lives in us</u>, and His love is made complete in us" (1 John 4:12).

Ephesians 5:1–2 teaches us how to *mimic God*. These verses state, "Be imitators of God, therefore, as dearly loved children, and live a life of love, just as Christ loved us and game Himself up for us as a fragrant offering and sacrifice to God."

How do we imitate God? The answer is, *by imitating Jesus Christ*. How do we do that? We do that by *walking in love*.

This can be summed up as love originating in God, love being manifested in His Son, Jesus Christ. Finally, we see His love in undeserved forgiveness. God's great proof of His love was sending His Son, Jesus Christ, to die for us. We show our love for God by how we treat His children. The sum of the Christian life is the reproduction of godliness as seen in the person of Jesus Christ. Imitating God's love is possible "because God has poured out His *love* into our hearts by the Holy Spirit, Whom He has given us" (Romans 5:5).

Love is sacrificially giving of yourself to others with no thought of return. In marriage, love is a total commitment to an imperfect person.

The following is the list of fifteen characteristics of love given in verb form, taken from 1 Corinthians 13 (NKJV):

1. "Love suffers long." It is the capacity to be patient with the pressure brought about by the one loved.
2. "Love is kind." It is the desire to bring about good to another.
3. "Love does not envy." This refers to both envy and jealousy. Envy desires to deprive someone of what they have. Jealousy wants to take it for oneself.
4. "Love does not parade itself." Love does not flaunt itself.
5. "Love is not puffed." True love is not proud.
6. "Love does not behave rudely." In other words, love does not behave with bad manners. Love is tactful and does not embarrass others.
7. "Love does not seek its own." Love is not self-centered. Love is not pre-occupied with ones' own interests.
8. "Love is not provoked." Love is not touchy or easily offended.
9. "Love thinks no evil." Love does not keep track of wrongs done by others.
10. "Love rejoices not in iniquity." Love is not happy when evil triumphs.
11. "Love rejoices in the truth." Love never overlooks, avoids, or compromises with error.
12. "Love bears all things." Love does not gossip. Love covers rather than broadcasting.
13. "Love believes all things." Love believes the best rather than believes the worst about other people.

14. "Love hopes all things." Love is optimistic. Love sees the bright side of situations.
15. "Love endures all things."

CHAPTER FIVE

Second Coming

"Multitudes who sleep in the dust of the earth will awake: some to everlasting life, others to shame and everlasting contempt." (Daniel 12:2)

I have been in discussion more than a few times concerning the Second Coming of Christ. All kinds of words come out, for instance: Amillennialism, Premillennialism, Postmillennialism, Day of the Lord, Preterism, Rapture, Tribulation, and many others. I have read through many books on the Second Coming: Theodore Epp, Hal Lindsey, Salem Kirban, John MacArthur, David Jeremiah, and others. I have been influenced by their writing. The following is my order of events of the Second Coming, thus far:

1. The Rapture
2. The Tribulation: Seven Years (Daniel and Revelation)
3. Armageddon: The Great Battle
4. The Coming of Christ
5. The Millennium: One Thousand–Year reign of Christ
6. The Great White Throne Judgment

7. The Casting of the Unrighteous into hell
8. Eternity

I am convinced of the following:

1. Concerning the first advent: the suffering servant (Bethlehem) and all the many prophecies that were fulfilled. It all worked out right to the tee.
2. Concerning the second advent (The Coming King): it will all be worked out right to the tee biblically. (There will be no committee that decides what the order of events and timing will be.) It is all planned by God.

Instead of spending all my time discussing and arguing over the *timing and order of the Second Coming*, I am determined to spend my time in helping fulfill the Great Commission. "Then Jesus came to them and said, 'All authority in heaven and on earth has been given to Me. Therefore go and make disciples of all nations, baptizing them in the name of the Father and of the Son and of the Holy Spirit, and teaching them to obey every thing I have commanded you. And surely I am with you always, to the very end of the age'" (Matthew 28:18–20).

The Great Commission is to "make disciples" by the following:

1. *Reaching* them with the Gospel (Christ died for our sin).
2. *Beaching* them (baptize by immersion, the first-century follow-up).
3. *Teaching* them the Word (worship, fellowship, evangelism, etc.).

I seek for balance in my Christian life. I seek to gain the following three things:

1. My goal is to have Christ to say to me: "Well done, good and faithful servant of Mine," *not* what others think about me. My goal is to do my good works motivated by *love*.

    The Greek language has four different words that are actually translated into the single English word "love." The following are descriptions of these Greek words:

    Eros: desiring romantic, sexual love. (This word is not used in the New Testament.)

    Philia: brotherly love and the love of friendship.

    Storge: love of family.

    Agape: the love that is of and from God, whose very nature is love itself. It is the love that seeks and works to meet another's highest welfare. It may involve emotion, but it *must* involve action. Love is not spiritual goose bumps, but moral obedience.

2. As a pastor, I must stand before God and give an account for my family (not where I have taken my Sunday school attendance, church growth, books I have written and so forth). (Noah preached for 120 years and had no converts. Yet he saved his family.)

3. As Christians, we are building our capacity to enjoy fellowship with Christ down here on earth (our works motivated by love to Christ and to others). Everyone should have a full cup of fellowship with Christ, *yet there are different-sized cups*. You are preparing your size of cup down here by your deeds motivated by love. Ephesians 2:8–9 says, "For it is by grace you have been saved, through faith, and this not from yourselves, it is the gift of God, not by works, so that no one can boast." You cannot earn your way to heaven. It is a gift. Once you receive this gift by faith, you celebrate your good works motivated by love. Ephesians 2:10 says, "For we are 'God's workmanship, created in Christ Jesus to do good works, which God prepared in advance for us to do.'"

CHAPTER SIX

Death

"Just as man is destined to die once, and after that to face judgment . . ." (Hebrews 6:27)

D eath is God's plan. We don't like to think about dying. But in reality, we must face it. We walk down the lanes of a cemetery where we learn that death comes to all: young and old. I remember the many times I spent with my mother while she was watering flowers at the grave of my brother Kenny. I do remember viewing the grave stones of the young children. They all looked alike. I noticed the neatly cut grass at the cemetery. My mother grieved over the death of my brother for years. I have learned that a mother losing a child is the greatest tragedy of all deaths.

All kinds of questions arise concerning death. Tennyson wrote of "crossing the bar." Is there a shadowy river to cross? Why is there a river and how does one cross it? We sing songs about "meeting beyond the river." What does "rest in peace" (RIP) really mean? What does it feel like to die?

I believe it is true that people are afraid of death because they do not know God. For a child of God, the fear of death has been removed. It disappeared. For a non-Christian, the fear of death is devastating and fearful. With God, we can look upon death from His standpoint. It is not "the end" but the beginning. It is not a failure but a success. Until then, we can live our lives fruitfully, knowing that when death comes knocking at our door it can be a glorious transition from one world to the next. Death becomes a graduation.

What really is death? *Death is separation.* William Orr has identified three types of death mentioned in the Bible:

1. *Physical Death*: Separation of the soul from the body. The nerves, muscles, bones, and blood remains. But no animation (John 11:11–14).
2. *Spiritual Death*: This is the separation of a human being from God (Ephesians 2:1).
3. *Eternal Death*: A never–ending exclusion from life, love, light, friends, and happiness. If a man bypasses the cross of Christ, hell will be his destiny (Revelation 20:13–14).

We can observe what will happen on this side of death, the earthly side is not pleasant. Life ebbs, the patient enters his deathbed, and the last breath is drawn.

Titanic: Amateurs built the ark. Professionals built the Titanic.

I have watched two films on the *Titanic*: *A Night to Remember* (1958) and *The Titanic* (1999). As you recall, in 1912, the *Titanic* collided with an iceberg and sank in about four hours. Of the 2,223 people on board, 1,517 perished. After I viewed both films, I would imagine what it would be like if I were present on that night in the Atlantic. It was cold, dark, and foreboding. People were screaming everywhere. It would have been dreadful! What would I have done? There are many stories about those few hours. I read about the string quartet musicians that kept playing as the ship was sinking. One of the tunes they played was "Nearer My God to Thee." Conflicting reports came out. Were they playing the tune that is familiar to us by Sarah Adams and Lowell Mason or another version? It does not really matter. Much has been written about those and similar incidents. This one thing I am certain about. No one wrote about rearranging the furniture. What is the use of rearranging the furniture on the *Titanic*? It is going down! It is fruitless.

Folks are carefully planning for retirement and are securing insurance on their boats, cars, homes, health, and life. And well they should be. The book of Proverbs says in chapter 6, verses 6 and 8: "Go to the ant, you sluggard; consider its ways and be wise!…it stores provisions in the summer and gathers its food at the harvest." The ant is an example of planning and serves as a rebuke to a person who does not prepare for the future. But people fail to make any provision for where they will spend eternity. Think of it! That is just like rearranging the furniture on the *Titanic*. It is going down.

Hebrews 2:14–15 says, "Since the children have flesh and blood, He too shared in their humanity so that by His death He might destroy him who holds the power of death, that is, the devil, and free those who all their lives were held in slavery by their *fear of death*."

Sir Francis Bacon concluded, "Men fear death, as children fear to go in the dark."

William Shakespeare wrote, "Cowards die many times before their deaths. The valiant never taste death but once."

Actor *Kirk Douglas*, who is a stroke overcomer, wrote a book called *"A Stroke of Luck."* He wrote that since his stroke, he has thought a lot about dying. He recalls fellow actors who have died. We can all recall many friends and relatives who have died.

We ask the question: "What happens after death?"

The answer to our question: "What happens after death?" is found in the book *One Heartbeat Away* by Mark Cahill.

God knows the day you were born and the day you will die. Your time on earth is finite and fleeting. It has a definite limit. But your time is infinite when you walk out of here. What are you going to do with your time here to ensure that your eternity is a joy?

Charles Spurgeon said, "Heaven and hell are not far away. You may be in heaven before the clock ticks again. It is so near. Oh, that we, instead of trifling about such things because they seem so far away, would solemnly realize them, since they are so very near! This very day, before the sun goes down, some here now sitting in this place may see the realities of heaven or hell. One of the most amazing things to do is to read what people said right before they died. The last statement they made with their very last breath. You can learn a great deal about what was important to these people by reading what they said. And it might give you some insight into what may have been in store for them after they took that last breath."

The following quotes by famous people, spoken on their death-beds, were collected by author *Mark Cahill.*

Cardinal Borgia: "I have provided in the course of my life for everything except death, and now alas, I am to die unprepared."

Elizabeth I: "All my possessions for one moment of time."

Thomas Hobbs (Atheist author of *Leviathan*, written to justify the rule of absolute monarchs and the oppression of the people): "I am about to take my last voyage; a great leap in the dark."

Anne Boleyn (wife of Henry VIII, who had her executed): "O God, have pity on my soul. O God, have pity on my soul."

Henry, Prince of Wales: "Tie a rope round my body, pull me out of bed, and lay me in ashes, that I may die with repentant prayers to an offended God. O! I in vain wish for that time I lost with you and others in vain recreations."

Socrates: "All of the wisdom of this world is but a tiny raft upon which we must set sail when we leave this earth. If only there was a firmer foundation upon which to sail, perhaps some divine word."

Tony Hancock (British comedian): "Nobody will ever know I existed. Nothing to pass on. Nobody to mourn me. That's the bitter-est blow of all."

Voltaire (Skeptic philosopher): "I am abandoned by God and man! I will give you half of what I am worth if you will give me six months of life. Then I shall go to hell; and you will go with me. O Christ! O Jesus Christ!"

James Dean (actor): "My fun days are over."

Jonathan Edwards (evangelist): "Trust in God and you shall have nothing to fear."

D. L. Moody (evangelist): "I see earth receding; heaven is opening. God is calling me."

Martin Luther: "Into Thy hands I commend my spirit! Thou hast redeemed me, O God of truth."

John Milton (British poet): "Death is the great key that opens the palace of Eternity."

Billy Graham said in an article called "Time and Eternity," "Life is like a shadow, like a fleeting cloud moving across the face of the sun."

David said, "We are aliens and stranger in your sight" (1 Chronicles 29:15). The world is *not* our permanent home; it is only temporary . . . How different would today be if you knew it would be your last one on earth before meeting God face-to-face? We should strive to live every day as it if was our last, for one day it will be! The Bible teaches that God knows the exact moment when each person is to die (Job 14:5). "Man's days are determined; You have decreed the number of his months and have set limits he cannot exceed."

Here is a portion of my personal testimony that I composed after my stroke:

John 12:24 says: "Very truly I tell you, unless a kernel of wheat falls to the ground and dies, it remains only a single seed. But if it dies, it produces many seeds." This verse is a picture of Christ dying for our sins and rising again. I could have died on January 16, 20017, when I had a stroke. But we are all going to eventually die. For example, in just a matter of years, there will be a notice in the obituary column of my death or of your death. At the funeral, someone might say, "He looks peaceful," or "He looks like his dad." Americans spend countless millions of dollars annually on various anti-aging products that claim to cure all sorts of things. But these cannot keep them from the inevitable: death.

My parents were brought up Lutheran. I was raised in the Christian and Missionary Alliance (The Hawley Bible Church). I went to a Methodist Church occasionally. I went to an Evangelical Free Church in college and graduate school. I attended a Baptist seminary and I married a former Catholic, who at one time wanted to be a nun.

It is *not* a religion or a denomination that saves us. Rather, the Gospel (the truth that Christ died for our sins and rose again) is what saves us.

Consider the following differences between religion and the Gospel:

Religion	*Gospel*
Whitewashes	Washes White
Is reformation	Is regeneration
Is rules and traditions	Is a Person: Jesus Christ
Reaches up to heaven	Is God reaching down to man
Says, "I am doing."	Says, "It is done."
Human accomplishment	Divine achievement
Man's work	God's grace

For instance, if I live to be the ripe old age of ninety-nine, I will have slept for thirty-three years of my life. Add to that the time spent waiting in line, shaving, getting stuck in traffic, getting over illness, listening to boring people, etc.

How much pure pleasure can be milked out of our existence? Then you come to eternity. Eternity lasts an awful long time.

Erwin W. Lutzer says in his book, *One Minute After You Die,* "How long is eternity? Visualize a bird coming to earth every million years and taking one grain of sand to a distant planet. At that rate, it would take thousands of billions of years before the bird had carried away a single handful of sand. Now let's expand that illustration and think how long it would take the bird to move the Oak Street Beach in Chicago and then the other thousands of beaches around the world. After that, the bird could begin on the mountains and the earth's crust. By the time the bird transported the entire earth to the far-off planet, eternity would not have officially begun. Strictly speaking, one cannot begin an infinite series, for a beginning implies an end. In other words, we might say that after the bird has done his work, those in eternity will not be one step closer to having their suffering alleviated. There is no such thing as half an eternity . . . Eternity endures, and it endures forever."

Death comes to Old Testament characters, like: Moses: "God buried him" (Deuteronomy 32:48–52); King Hezekiah (2 Kings 20:1–21); Onan (Genesis 38:10), Saul (1 Samuel 28:18–19); King David's infant son (2 Samuel 12–14); Sennacherib (2 Kings 19:7, 33, 37); and Babylon's King Belshazzar (Daniel 5:26–30).

In the New Testament, death comes to characters like Ananias and Sapphira (Acts 5:1–11), Stephen, the first martyr (Acts 7:54–60); Paul, in the letter to Timothy (2 Timothy 4:6–8); Peter (2 Peter 4:14, Berkeley): "I know that my tent will be struck as our Lord Jesus Christ made clear to me."

Death occurs to infants, youth, and people in midlife, and to people of all ages. Two deaths are very interesting: Lazarus and Paul; Lazarus died and was resurrected by the hand of God (John 11:1–46). Many biblical lessons are learned by reading John 11. Paul had a mysterious first death. (Read the chapter on heaven: chapter 7.)

Christ's Death

I was inspired by Russel B. Jones when he wrote the book *Gold from Golgotha* (1945, out of print).

The seven last words from the Cross:

Golgotha is the focal point of revelation, history, and experience. God did His best here while man did his worst. *We best see God by watching Jesus die.*

1. "Father, forgive them, for they do not know what they are doing." He kept on saying it (Greek: continuous action).
2. "Today you will be with me in Paradise." Both thieves kept on making their requests: one a temporal request, one an eternal request.
3. "Dear woman, here is your son . . . Here is your mother." Like all the words from the cross, the full meaning of this third word had to wait for the Resurrection and Pentecost.
4. "My God, My God, why have You forsake Me?" The most mysterious of all the words coming from the cross.

   - There was darkness upon the earth for three hours (twelve to three o'clock). It was fitting that the *sun* should be darkened while the *Son* suffered.
   - The mockery had doubtless died from the lips of the crowd, a strange fear and awe had come to birth in everyone's heart, and the deep silence was broken only by the difficulty breathing and groaning from the victims.
   - This scene gives us insight into Christ's sacrifice, hell's torment, and God's wrath on sin.

5. "After this, Jesus knowing that all things were accomplished, that the scripture might be fulfilled, saith, 'I thirst.'"

   - This cry reminds us that our Lord Jesus shared our human nature and its infirmities. "Both the one who makes men holy and those who are made holy are of the same family. So Jesus is not ashamed to call them brothers" (Hebrews 2:11).

- This cry is an evidence of our Lord's extreme humiliation. He who had turned the water into wine and had miraculously fed about twenty thousand people using five biscuits and two small fish now begged for a little water.

- Actually by expressing His thirst He was doing two very definite things:

   First: He was announcing Himself as the Victor exhausted from the conflict.

   Second: He was identifying Himself as the Savior promised in the scriptures.

   "After this . . . that the scripture might be fulfilled (He) saith, 'I thirst.'"

   He had won the victory and now He was thirsty, which leads to the sixth word.

6. "When He had received the drink, Jesus said, 'It is finished.'"

- The predictions referring the the Messiah were now fulfilled: "The seed of the woman shall bruise the serpent's head."

   "It pleased the Lord to bruise him."
   "The Messiah shall be cut off."
   "I will smite the Shepherd."

- The obedience and humiliation of the Son of God were now completed.

   "He learned obedience by the things which He suffered." (Hebrews 5)

- The sacrifice of the Lamb of God was accomplished.
- While 250,000 lambs were being slaughtered in Jerusalem for the Passover, outside the city, hung the Lamb of God, dying for the sins of the world.

"The high priest carries the blood of animals into the most holy place as a sin offering, but the bodies are burned outside the camp. And so Jesus also suffered outside the city gate to make the people holy through His own blood. Let us, then, go to Him outside the camp, bearing the disgrace He bore. For here we do not have an enduring city, but we are looking for the city that is to come." (Hebrews 13:11–14)

- The Greek word, "tetelastai," means "It is finished."

F. W. Boreham in *A Handful of Stars* catches the spirit of the word *tetelestai*. "And when, in the fullness of time, the Lamb of God offered Himself on the altar of the ages, He rejoiced with a joy so triumphant that it bore down all His anguish before it. The sacrifice was stainless, perfect, finished! He cried with a loud voice, 'Tetelestai!' and gave up the ghost."

7. "Father, into your hands I commit my spirit."

- Jesus gave up His life because He willed it, when He willed it, and as He willed it (Augustine). In this victorious, vicarious, voluntary word, we see Jesus as man's: Prophet, Priest, and King.

Funerals

"Precious in the sight of the Lord is the death of His faithful servants." (Psalms 116:15)

I remember attending funerals when I was young. My first funeral, however, I didn't attend. It was at my brother's funeral. (I was not yet two years old.) My older sister and my older brother and I stayed home. (Actually, we wandered about town, population 1,500. From store to store, people felt sorry for us and gave us candy.) My older brother Kenny, age sixteen, died as a result of a tumor in his brain which was caused by an injury to his head when he was playing football. (I remember seeing his tombstone out in the car before it was hauled out to the cemetery.)

Since that time I sang at many, many funerals, and conducted funerals in my thirty-five years as a pastor. I remember singing such songs as "Beyond the Sunset" and "Going Down the Valley." My "ideal" funeral is for an older saint who served Jesus all his or her life. It was a celebration. And I remember sad funerals: suicides and young children.

As a pastor, funerals are usually hard (visitation, counseling, and planning the funeral.) As a pastor, I learned one thing: you don't have to get their attention when delivering the sermon. You already have it.

There are individuals who are weeping. Some others are there out of duty. A few are there to get a free meal. (I heard about a person who for thirty-seven years never ate at home. He survived eating at funerals.) But there are two kinds of people in attendance. Those on the way to heaven and those on the way to hell. That's why the one delivering the sermon must be articulate. The sermon is all-inclusive. They must include a note of comfort and the gospel. *People must hear the Gospel.* The gospel is: "Christ died and rose again for the sins of humanity." The ones attending the funeral are faced with the fact that they will eventually have to die themselves. Talk about an attention-getting experience! At death, the die has been cast. It has all been decided. Folks may remark: "They are in a better place." But are they really? What happens when we die?

In the Old Testament, there is a place called Sheol. In the New Testament, it is called Hades. It is the same place. The words are basically synonymous (Sheol-Hades). Both those in heaven and Hades are there in an intermediate, spirit, bodiless state. This state is both conscious and immediate upon death. No matter what the preacher says, or the one eulogy speaker remembers, the bottom line is, "What does God say?"

"What will you do with Jesus?"
-     Neutral you cannot be.
One day your heart will be asking
What will He do with me?" (A. B. Simpson)
What will Jesus do with me? That is the only question!

The Rich Man and Lazarus

"There was a rich man who was dressed in purple and fine linen and lived in luxury every day. At his gate was laid a beggar named Lazarus, covered with sores and longing to eat what fell from the rich man's table. Even the dogs came and licked his sores.

"The time came when the beggar died and the angels carried him to Abraham's side. The rich man also died and was buried. In Hades, where he was in torment, he looked up and saw Abraham far away, with Lazarus by his side. So he called to him, 'Father Abraham, have pity on me and send Lazarus to dip the tip of his finger in water and cool my tongue, because I am in agony in this fire.'

"But Abraham replied, 'Son, remember that in your lifetime you received your good things, while Lazarus received bad things, but now he is comforted here and you are in agony. And besides all this, between us and you a great chasm has been set in place, so that those who want to go from here to you cannot, nor can anyone cross over from there to us.'

"He answered, 'Then I beg you, father, send Lazarus to my family, for I have five brothers. Let him warn them, so that they will not also come to this place of torment.'

"Abraham replied, 'They have Moses and the Prophets; let them listen to them.'

"'No, father Abraham,' he said, 'but if someone from the dead goes to them, they will repent.'

"He said to him, 'If they do not listen to Moses and the Prophets, they will not be convinced even if someone rises from the dead.'"

The Lord Himself told this story. Actually, it is not a parable, but a case history of the death of two men. They represent (illustrate) two different men and two different destinations.

First man: The first man was rich—garbed in purple and linen (wealth and position). Perhaps gluttony hastened his death.

Second man: The second man was a beggar filled with running ulcers, which were licked by many street dogs. Apparently, no one cared for him.

First man: He died perhaps with pomp and ceremony, hired mourners, perhaps *with perfume, spices, etc. He was buried perhaps in a grand tomb.*

Second man: He also died. Perhaps he was tossed in an unmarked pile, which was to feed the wild dogs and vultures.

The beggar was carried by the angels into Abrahams's bosom, into the immediate presence of the patriarch. The rich man, himself, was in the torment of Hades. (The Greek equivalent of the Old Testament word Sheol.) The place of the departed spirit was in two divisions. The place of the righteous dead: Paradise. And the place of the unrighteous dead: Hades, in torment.

They are separated by a chasm. Neither of them can cross over to the other side. (Now, Paradise and heaven are synonymous.) The unsaved dead remain in the lower Sheol or Hades.

Both of these men were dead, but they remain conscious. Their physical bodies were still on earth. The beggar was comforted, happy, and satisfied. The rich man was being tormented and begged for a drop of water to cool him.

Both men experienced immediate transition from the earth's sphere to another realm (a temporary body or spirit body). For a Christian, the new body provides a new spirit body (1 Corinthians 15:44). For a Christian, this body house is the one spoke of as "A building of God" (2 Corinthians 5:1).

Both men can see, feel, speak, hear, recognize, and reason. The point is they are in two different places for eternity. When both men died, it was the end of their earthly life, but not the end of their next life. It was only the beginning.

William Orr writes from the booklet *The First Five Minutes After Death*, "The enduring lessons of this account are both negative and positive. There is no 'valley of the shadow' here, no 'soul sleeping,' no crossing of dark rivers, no wandering of the departed souls in abysmal emptiness. The apostle Peter is not stationed at any gate of entrance. The court of God has not yet convened. Torment is real: Hades is dreadfully solitary. There is no second chance anywhere."

Paul's first death? The Scripture contains a mystery. Most Bible scholars state that Paul died via stoning at the town named Lystra during his first missionary journey. Stoning was an ugly sight. The stones weighed about two pounds. Rarely did anyone come through a stoning alive. There is every reason to believe that he died.

"Then some Jews came from Antioch and Iconium and won the crowd over. They stoned Paul and dragged him out of the city, thinking he was dead. But after the disciples had gathered around him, he got up and went back into the city. The next day he and Barnabas left for Derbe" (Acts 14:19–20). What had happened?

"I know a man in Christ who fourteen years ago was caught up to the third heaven. Whether it was in the body or out of the body I do not know—God knows. And I know that this man—whether in the body or apart from the body I do not know, but God knows—was caught up to paradise and heard inexpressible things, things that no one is permitted to tell. I will boast about a man like that, but I will not boast about myself, except about my weaknesses. Even if I should choose to boast, I would not be a fool, because I would be speaking the truth. But I refrain, so no one will think more of me than is warranted by what I do or say, or because of these surpassingly great revelations. Therefore, in order to keep me from becoming conceited, I was given a thorn in my flesh, a messenger of Satan, to torment me. Three times I pleaded with the Lord to take it away from me. But he said to me, "My grace is sufficient for you, for my power is made perfect in weakness." Therefore I will boast all the more gladly about my weaknesses, so that Christ's power may rest on me. That is why, for Christ's sake, I delight in weaknesses, in insults, in hardships, in persecutions, in difficulties. For when I am weak, then I am strong." (2 Corinthians 12:2–10)

This had occurred about ten years before the epistle was written (2 Corinthians 2–10). It seemed like a dream or a vision. But I think he actually experienced it. After he stopped breathing, he entered into the heavenly experience. Paul says that he did not know whether he was in the body or out of it.

William Orr states that "Many believe that the Lord provides a temporary body for a child of God until he receives his glorified body" (2 Corinthians 5:1–5). If so, Paul was able instantly to see, to hear, and to enjoy the indescribable, glorious sight of heaven. He heard things and saw scenes that are indescribable. In fact, he said they were so sacred that it should be unlawful to describe them. All of this took place in a brief amount of time."

What was a thorn in the flesh? My opinion is that Paul had an eye problem caused by stoning. He prayed three times that the thorn would be removed.

Paul's last death: Again, William Orr writes the following: "We have no record of Paul's second death. Most likely he was beheaded in Rome. Moreover, Paul was not dying: he was departing. The term he uses is a nautical one. The ship that had anchored so long in the harbor of earth would draw up the anchor and hoist its sails. Soon it would glide off into God's boundless eternity. There awaited thrilling new experiences and a new universe to explore."

Chapter Seven

Heaven

"Do not let your hearts be troubled. You believe in God; believe also in me. My Father's house has many rooms; if that were not so, would I have told you that I am going there to prepare a place for you? And if I go and prepare a place for you, I will come back and take you to be with me that you also may be where I am." (John 14:1–3)

I have found that you don't commit intellectual suicide by studying the Bible. I ask three questions concerning Scripture:

1. *What?* What does it say in its grammatical and historic setting?
2. *So What?* What is the meaning upon careful examination?
3. *Now What?* What does God want me to do in the light of the Scripture just studied?

So I come to the consideration about heaven.

1. Figure of Speech: All kinds of Scriptures contain "figures of speech."

    a. Christ is called a door.
    b. Christ is called the bread and wine.
    c. Peter is called a rock.
    d. "Look, the Lamb of God" (John 1) (Jesus was not a literal lamb. He did not have wool or four legs.)
    e. Laodicea is being lukewarm? (Revelation 3).
    f. Is Christ the Lion of Judah? etc.

2. Literally speaking:

    a. Multiplying loaves and fishes.
    b. Healing people.
    c. Calming the storm.
    d. Crossing the Red Sea.
    e. Christ is being crucified, etc.

Heaven

    a. was created by God,
    b. is everlasting,
    c. is immeasurable,
    d. is high,
    e. is holy.

God

    a. is the Lord of heaven,
    b. reigns in heaven,
    c. dwells in heaven,
    d. has His throne in heaven,
    e. fills heaven,
    f. answers His people from heaven,
    g. sends His judgments from heaven.

John MacArthur described heaven on one of his tapes as follows:

'Heaven will be perfect freedom from all evil forever. Never a sinful thought. Never a selfish thought. Never an evil deed. Never a useless word. Never imperfect. Always doing everything which is perfect and holy. No doubts, no fear of God's displeasure. No temptation. No persecution. No abuse. No division. No discord. No disharmony. No disunity. No disappointments. No anger. No effort. No prayer (there will be nothing to pray for). No fasting (there will be nothing to fast for). No repentance (there will be nothing to repent of). No confessions (there won't be any sin). No weeping (there will be nothing to make you sad). No watchfulness (there will be no danger). No trials. No teaching, no preaching, no learning (we'll have all spiritual understanding and there will be nothing to learn). No evangelism or witnessing. Perfect pleasure. Perfect knowledge. Perfect comfort. We will love as Jesus loved, absolutely and perfectly. And we will have perfect, complete, unending joy.

In heaven we'll never have to apologize, we'll never have to confess, we'll never feel bad. We'll never have to make any corrections, never have to clarify, never have to explain what we really meant, and we'll never have to straighten anything out from confusion because nothing will ever be confused. We won't have to fix anything, repair anything, adjust anything because nothing will ever wear out or malfunction. Never have to help anybody, nobody will need help. Won't have to deal with satan, demons, or sinners. Won't have to defend ourselves, there will be no attack. We'll never cry, never be alone, never be lonely, never be hurt emotionally or physically. We will never have to be cured, counseled, coddled or entertained. We'll always be filled with joy. Never have to do anything special for anybody because everything we do will be special to everyone all the time. There will never be any grief. We'll never lose anything, never miss anyone, and we won't have to be careful because we won't ever make a mistake. We won't have to plan for contingencies or emergencies, because there will never be a Plan B. We'll never have to avoid danger because there will be no danger.

Heaven is the experience of eternal perfection of body and soul. (From *Playing the Odds* by Jay Carty)

I have many questions about heaven. I do not drink alcohol. Do we actually drink wine in heaven? What is the cuisine during the Marriage Feast of the Lamb? Will we grow intellectually in heaven? What language will we speak? What is the tonality of singing and what kinds of instruments (if any) will we play? Will there be animals in heaven? As a singer, will I maintain my lyrical tenor voice or will I be a bass singer? What will family relationships be like? Is there any coffee in heaven? Will there be any golf in heaven? How about children that have been miscarried or aborted? How about sleep? How will heaven be like earth in music we love or DNA we have been born with? *How much carryover from earth to heaven will there be?*

And finally, one more question about heaven. "How will it feel to be happy all the time?" Three cases in point:

1. You take a good, hot shower. It feels wonderful, *but* it was preceded by feeling hot and sticky.
2. What is the key to good eating? Answer: *hunger*. I remember years ago working with my two older brothers, loading scrap iron out in the country. We had miscalculated how long it would take to load the junk into a large truck. It was

about 3:00 p.m., and we were hungry. We didn't bring our lunch. Personally, I was so hungry that eating grass looked appetizing. The old farmer said, "Do you want something to eat?" We said, "YES!" So the farmer ushered us into his small farmhouse. As I recall, the house had a dirt floor. He served us cold cheese sandwiches. (I hated cold cheese sandwiches.) He also served Fig Newtons. (I hated Fig Newtons.) He gave us some coffee. *I never enjoyed eating so much in my life.* That was because I was so hungry.

3. Have you ever been really thirsty? I have. Then you finally drink from a well and you quench your thirst and WOW!

This is a case in point: In heaven, there will be no *thirst*, no need to *shower*, no *hunger*. Wouldn't the law of diminishing returns be activated?

Years ago, I was teaching a Sunday school class in Grand Forks, ND. The same question came up. "Won't it be boring in heaven to be happy all the time?" I answered this way: "The thrill of being happy all the time would be in getting happier and happier—*all the time*. Like a crescendo in music, getting *louder and louder*." I do not worry about these questions. I just wonder?

I do believe one thing: Heaven will *not* be boring. It will not be like a child enduring a long church service where they sing all the verses starting on page 1, in a slow tempo, and a long sermon on the whole book of Leviticus spoken in Hebrew, daydreaming that he is floating on a cloud and learning to play the harp, desperately waiting for church service to be over and to hear the Benediction!

When I think about heaven, I think: "How exciting it will be." I think growing in heaven, serving in some capacity, meeting and having fellowship with new people. I dream of shaking Paul's hand. I would like to ask Jonah, "What was it like in the belly of a big fish?" But first of all, I will meet Jesus Christ, my Savior!

The person who has departed this life will be completely conscious, alert, and aware of everything that is happening to him. I quote William Orr, "For a Christian, the moment of death is the doorway into a new, glorious life that will NEVER end . . . Fellowship will be the occupation of heaven. We will actually see God. In fact, the triune God-Father, Son, and Holy Spirit—will dwell with us and we with Him. We will be privileged to wear His Name on our foreheads. Walking by faith will graduate into walking by sight."

Randy Alcorn writes: "God is grooming us for leadership. He's watching to see how we demonstrate our faithfulness. Christ is not simply preparing a place for us; He is preparing a place for us; He is preparing us for that place. We'll have more work, more responsibilities, increased opportunities, along with greater abilities, resources, wisdom, and empowerment. We will have sharp minds, strong bodies, clear purpose, and unabated joy. The more we serve Christ now, the greater our capacity will be to serve Him in heaven."

Chapter Eight

Hell

"Then death and Hades were thrown into the lake of fire. The lake of fire is the second death. Anyone whose name was not found written in the book of life was thrown into the lake of fire." (Revelation 20:14–15)

"Hell disappeared and no one noticed," C. S. Lewis wrote. "The safest road to hell is a gradual one—the gentle slope, soft, underfoot, without sudden turning, without milestone, without signposts."

Newsweek Magazine printed: "Today, hell is a theological 'h' word, a subject too trite for serious scholarship." Gordon Kaufman at Harvard Divinity School, says, "I don't think there can be any future for heaven or hell."

I grew up in church. Hawley Bible Church of the Christian and Missionary Alliance was only one block from my home. I used to travel to attend church, at least five times a week (Sunday school, Sunday morning, and Sunday evening services, youth service, and Wednesday evening service, along with Vacation Bible School, special meetings, tent meetings, and church cleaning). Whenever the church was open, I was in it. (For seventeen years until I entered college.)

I remember sermons on the Second Coming and sermons on heaven and hell. I grew up with such preaching. After I became a pastor, I have studied heaven and hell in detail for my preaching services and counseling. I conclude my thoughts in the following: "There's nothing so exactly opposite than heaven and hell." You study in detail of the glorious reality Heaven and the hopeless, awfulness of hell—well, you get the picture.

I would like to turn my thoughts about hell through what others say about hell:

Here's an unknown writer's opinion of hell: "There is no way to describe hell. Nothing on earth can compare with it. No living person has any real idea of it. No madman in his wildest flights of insanity ever beheld its horror. No man in delirium ever pictured a place so utterly terrible as this. No nightmare racing across some fevered mind has ever produced a terror to match even the mildest hell. No murder scene with splashed blood and oozing wound ever suggested revulsion that could touch the borderlines of hell. Let the most gifted writer exhaust his skill in describing this roaring cavern of unending flame and he would not even brush in fancy the nearest edge of hell."

Quote from the Zondervan Pictorial Bible Dictionary (Zondervan Publishing House 1963):

"Life apart from God is existence filled with guilt, hollowness, despair, meaningless, and helplessness. The agony of eternal punishment apparently involves both body and soul because Scripture says both are ultimately cast into hell. Apparently this would involve inner anguish as well as detrimental effects upon the body. It may involve the torment of being cut off from fellowship with one's fellow man, and also the results of living within a society of men from which the grace of God has been completely withdrawn."

John MacArthur says, "Perhaps no doctrine is harder to accept emotionally than the doctrine of hell. Yet it is too clear and too often mentioned in the Scripture either to deny or ignore. Jesus spoke more of hell than any of the prophets or apostles did—perhaps for the reason that its horrible truth would be all but impossible to accept had not the Son of God Himself absolutely affirmed it. It had special emphasis in Jesus' teaching from the beginning to the end of His earthly ministry. He said more about hell than about love. More than all the other teachers in the Bible combined. He warned men of hell, promising no escape for those who refused His gracious, loving offer of salvation.

"Hell is a place of constant torment, misery, pain. The torment is often described as darkness (Matthew 22:13), where no light can penetrate, and nothing can be seen. Throughout the numberless eons of eternity, the damned will never again see light or anything that light illumines. Hell's torment is also described as fire that will never go out and cannot be extinguished (Mark 9:43) and from which the damned will never find relief. Hell could not be other than the place where there shall be weeping and gnashing of teeth.

Hell will involve the torment of both body and soul. Neither the soul nor the body is annihilated at death: nor will they ever be. The torment of hell will be everlasting. Nothing will be so horrible about hell as its endlessness."

Hell

Novelist Dorothy Sayers writes, "There seems to be a kind of conspiracy to forget or to conceal, where the doctrine of hell is not 'medieval priestcraft' for frightening people into giving money to the church; it is Christ's deliberate judgment of sin. We cannot repudiate Hell without altogether repudiating Christ."

C. S. Lewis wrote of hell: "There is no doctrine which I would more willingly remove from Christianity than this, if it lay in my power. But it has full support of Scripture and, especially, of our Lord's own words; it has always been held by Christendom and it has the support of reason."

Scripture says of those who die without Christ: "They will be punished with everlasting destruction and shut out from the presence of the Lord and from the majesty of His power . . ." (2 Thessalonians 1:9).

Randy Alcorn says of hell: "Hell will have no community, no camaraderie, no friendship. More likely, each person is in solitary confinement. Hell will be agonizingly dull, small, and insignificant; without company, purpose, or accomplishment."

In Scripture, it says that there are two gates and two ways.

The *broad road* is the way of the ungodly, easy, attractive, indulgent, and permissive way of the world. Here is where "sin is tolerated, truth is moderated and humility is ignored." No moral character, no commitment, and no sacrifice. It is floating down the stream, sliding down a playground slide. It is, "the way which seems right to man" but whose "end is the way of death."

The way that is *narrow* is the way of self-denial, the cross, and total commitment. It is the way of poverty of the spirit, mourning over sin. The command is to enter this gate now, because "today is the day of salvation." (2 Corinthians 6:2) We must enter alone through a turnstile. The narrow gate is through Jesus Christ. "I am the Way, the Truth, and the Life" (John 14:6).

Two destinations:

One destination leads to destruction, a wasted life, and to hell. (Not to extinction or annihilation, but to total ruin.)

The other destination leads to complete fulfillment, its benefits are "out of this world"—everlasting fellowship with God, His angels, and His people.

Two groups:

One group (a large group) who do not go through the gate, Jesus Christ. This group will be made up of atheists, agnostics, religionists, theists, and humanists, Jews, and Gentile—and nominal Christians who were never impregnated with Jesus Christ, never born from above.

The other group will be a small group. A small group, not because God's grace is limited, or that there is limited room in heaven, but because so few truly believe.

CHAPTER NINE

The Gospel

"For God so loved the world that he gave his one and only Son, that whoever believes in him shall not perish but have eternal life." (John 3:16)

"If you declare with your mouth, 'Jesus is Lord,' and believe in your heart that God raised him from the dead, you will be saved. For it is with your heart that you believe and are justified, and it is with your mouth that you profess your faith and are saved." (Romans 10:9–10)

"'By this gospel you are saved, if you hold firmly to the word I preached to you.' 'For what I received I passed on to you as of first importance: that Christ died for our sins according to the Scriptures, that he was buried, that he was raised on the third day according to the Scriptures, and that he appeared to Cephas, and then to the Twelve. After that, he appeared to more than five hundred of the brothers and sisters at the same time, most of whom are still living, though some have fallen asleep." (1 Corinthians 15:2a, 3–6)

The four verbs of the gospel:

a.   They came in pairs with the latter confirming the former. Christ *"died"* and was *"buried"* (burial confirms His death to be real), and He *"rose again"* and was *"seen"* (seeing Christ after His death confirms His resurrection).

b.   Note that one of these verbs has an attached prepositional phrase, "for our sins."

Christ *died* for our sins, was *buried*, *rose* again, was *seen*.

"for our sins."

The phrase *"for our sins"* does not go with all four verbs, only one. Atonement is effected by the death of Christ. The word *"for"* is from the Greek word, *huper*, and means on behalf of. Christ's death was a substitution for us. Our sin-guilt and punishment was borne by Him. This is obviously *euangelia*—good news! The term good news comes from the Greek word: *euangelia*.

"I am not ashamed of the gospel, because it is the power of God for the salvation of everyone who believes: first for the Jew, then for the Gentile." (Romans 1:16)

Here in the Midwest, as it is throughout the world, we deal with a society that is *incurably religious*. It's "Do" (work your way to salvation) vs. "Done" (Christ has already paid for your salvation).

Both you and I have a problem. We are sinners. To sin means to miss the mark, or standard, that God has set. Consider these statements from the Bible.

"For all have sinned and fall short of the glory of God." (Romans 3:23)

The penalty for sin is death (eternal spiritual separation from God).

"For the wages of sin is death, but the gift of
God is eternal life in Christ Jesus our Lord."
(Romans 6:23)

But there is Good News! Christ died for you and for me.

"But God demonstrates His own love for us in this: While we
were still sinners, Christ died for us." (Romans 5:8)

Christ took the penalty for our sin by dying in our place. Not
only did He die in our place, but He rose again from the dead. He
conquered death.

"For we know that since Christ was raised from the dead, He
cannot die again: death no longer has mastery over Him." (Romans
6:9)

You can be saved through faith in Christ.

"For it is by grace you have been saved, through faith, and this
is not from yourselves, it is the gift of God, not by works, so that no
one can boast." (Ephesians 2:8–9)

Faith simply means trust. You must trust in Christ alone to forgive you and to give you eternal life.

Think carefully. There is nothing more important that your
need to trust Christ.

Would you like to tell God you are trusting Jesus Christ as your
Savior? If you would, why not pray right now and tell God you are
trusting His Son?

It is not a prayer that saves you. It is trusting Jesus Christ that
saves you. The prayer is simply how you tell God what you are doing.

Dear God, I know I am a sinner. I know my sin deserves to be
punished. I believe Christ died for me and rose from the grave. I trust
Jesus Christ alone as my Savior. Thank you for the forgiveness and
everlasting life I now have. In Jesus's name. Amen

Someone has said, "The work of evangelism is not complete
until the convert is an active member of the body of Christ." I agree.

People may report there are many, many souls saved during a
crusade or special meetings. But how many were added to the church
family?

How many are soundly converted? Only eternity will tell.

For instance, a person prays the prayer of salvation, then what is next?

1. Start going to church where the gospel is preached, taught, and lived out.
2. Plan to be baptized (immersed).
3. Join a small group Bible study.
4. Join a ministry group, i.e., Stephen Ministry, Choir, Evangelism group, Alpha, Celebrate Recovery, Awana, etc.

In other words, grow and become a disciple in your church.

Though no one can go back and make a brand new start, anyone can start from now and make a brand new ending.

EPILOGUE 1

Incarnational Living

1. "I have been crucified with Christ and I no longer live, but Christ lives in me. The life I live in the body, I live by faith in the Son of God, Who loved me and gave Himself for me." (Galatians 2:20, NIV)

Christ living through us: *incarnational living*.

The definition of *incarnational living* is this: Christ living through us. "The true light "Jesus Christ" that gives light to everyone was coming into the world" (John 1:9). Connected to this concept is John 1:14, which says, "The Word (Jesus Christ) became flesh and made His dwelling among us. We have seen His glory, the glory of the one and only Son, Who came from the Father, full of grace and truth."

John MacArthur writes when commenting on John 1:18 in the NKJV: "No one has seen God at any time. The only begotten Son, Who is in the bosom of the Father, He has DECLARED Him. This term denotes the mutual intimacy, love and knowledge existing in the Godhead. Notice the term: 'DECLARED'. Theologians derived the term 'exegesis' or 'to interpret' from this word. John, the Apostle, meant that all Jesus is and does, interprets and explains Who God is and what He does."

2. "Be imitators of God, therefore, as dearly loved children and live a life of love, just as Christ loved us and gave Himself up for us as a fragrant offering and sacrifice to God." (Ephesians 5:1–2, NIV)

    We imitate God by imitating Jesus Christ. How? By walking in love. *Incarnational living.*

3. "For we are God's workmanship, created in Christ Jesus to do good works, which God prepared in advance for us to do" (Ephesians 2:10, NIV). Incarnational living.

4. I close my thoughts on Incarnational Living with my mom, who truly lived an *incarnational life.*

My mother, Jennie Louise Quam

This was written by my brother Butch:

It was the summer of 1949 and a hot, sweaty day. It was about ten o'clock in the morning. On old-looking man came walking up from the railroad track. He was about fifty-five or sixty years old. As he walked to our house, he looked like he was eighty years old. He was hot and dirty. He had an old pair of pants that needed washing badly. His shirt was tattered and too heavy for the kind of day, which only added to his odor. The shoes he wore were low dress shoes with holes in them, and he wore no socks.

He had a winter hat on and he was missing a number of teeth. My brother, sister, and I were used to seeing men like this every day, walking along the tracks. The term used to identify these people was "hobo," "bum," or "tramp." All these names have their own historical definitions, but to us they were all used interchangeably to describe the same individual.

The man came up to the back door of the house where some of my friends and I were playing. We all watched as he knocked on the door. Mom soon came to the door and locked it very noticeably. With all the strangers walking and riding the rails, Mom was very kind, but also very careful.

The man said to her, "Can I have a drink of water and a slice of bread?"

At this point in today's world, most people would tell the man to go to the local food pantry or go down to the mission, or maybe they would give him a diet Pepsi and a Twinkie. But the nearest mission was twenty-five miles away in Fargo, North Dakota, and in reality, the only food pantry in town was Mom Quam's kitchen. My friends used to come to our house to get their daily big slice of homemade bread with strawberry jam on it. My mom said, "Yes, I will get you something. Please sit down under that shade tree over there." At that point, she forgot what she was doing at the time, turned and began the task of preparing a meal for someone who could never give her anything in return. The task, to her, was like she was going to entertain the president of the United States, the king of Sweden, or the ing of Norway. My mom was half Swedish and half Norwegian.

At that time, I didn't question what motivated my mom to feed these people. It was just Mom and no one questioned her reasons for doing what she did, whether it was for her family, the pastor, Christian brothers and sisters, or the bums.

The first thing Mom did was to send me out with a glass of ice water in a large, colorful glass. He gulped it down, some of it spilling on his clothes.

When I went back into the house, I smelled one of the most endearing smells of my childhood, the making of a fried egg sandwich, as only Mom could make it. She used Uncle Norman Larson's fresh eggs from the farm where she was born and raised. The eggs were so big that some of them contained two yolks. She carefully put just enough salt and pepper on them, and of course, butter was used as a frying agent. Oh yes, and the yolks needed to be broken to make sure the egg was well done.

Next, she prepared the bread. The day before, she had baked bread, which is another story in itself. (I will always remember coming home from school, at least once a week, and smelling the bread from a distance of two blocks.) She used a large loaf of white bread, from which she cut two fairly thick slices and buttered them. By this time, the eggs were well done and the sandwich could now be assembled. She then cut the sandwich in three pieces.

I'm not exactly sure what the other items on the menu were, but a freshly baked white cake with thick chocolate frosting seems familiar. A large piece was cut. Also a large glass was poured full of cold milk. The next part of the story is important. Most people today would use paper plates, plastic forks, knives, and a paper cup, all of which would be disposed of in the nearest trash bin, upon completion of the meal. No housewife would risk losing regular tableware by letting a stranger use them.

But not Mom. She put the giant egg sandwich on a full-size plate, the best she had. The cake was on another plate and the milk was in the best large, decorative glass. These were all put on a tray, along with our best eating utensils and a couple of colorful napkins. She then sent me out with the tray to the place where the old man was sitting on the ground. You'll notice that nothing on the tray was hard to chew. Mom was considerate in giving the man only what he could chew with what teeth he had remaining.

The old fellow took the tray and began to wolf down the food. He wasted no time in satisfying his hunger, which many have gone on for a few days. His manners were horrible. But he was being fed with Mom's cooking and probably thought he had died and gone to heaven. I walked back into the house and guess what Mom was doing? She was preparing a lunch for the old man to take with him, as he would no doubt get hungry within a matter of hours. I don't recall what kind of sandwich it was, but I think it was cheese or jelly or maybe one of each. She also set aside and orange. The orange he could eat without the use of a lot of teeth. Mom's cookies were also there, probably oatmeal or peanut butter.

All the lunch was carefully wrapped in wax paper and put into a bag. What she did next was going the extra mile for this poor fellow. She took one of her precious two-quart Mason jars, filled it with water and put on the lid. Next she wrapped the jar using newspapers to serve as an insulating material. The lunch and jar of cold water were placed in a heavy-paper sugar bag. One other important item was put into the bag. Mom placed a Gospel of John very carefully in the bag. She knew that man needed spiritual food as well as her homemade bread.

Mom told me to take the bag of goodies out to the man and give it to him. She didn't even go out to the man to let him thank her. I guess she wanted God to get the glory for this act of kindness. He looked into the bag with a look of disbelief and said, "Thank you, thank you." As he walked down the road to the place where he could get on the railroad tracks, I wondered where he would go next or what he was thinking. My mom went back to her busy day washing clothes, baking bread and more cookies and watching her children. My dad would soon be home for the noon meal, probably consisting of mashed potatoes, Swedish meatballs, and gravy, creamed carrots, homemade brown bread, and apple pie, freshly baked.

My children love to have me tell them this story of "Grandma Feeding the Old Man." I've probably told it to them a hundred times. On occasion, they would ask the question, "Dad, was that old man an angel?" (Sometimes, God sends down angels disguised as various people for some special purpose.) My answer to them was, "We really don't know. When we get to heaven, we'll find out."

People ask me what training is needed to work in a rescue mission. The expected answer might be from an assortment of work experiences and/or academic degrees. These are important. My training came in watching my Mother feed an old man and giving him the Gospel, when I was nine years old.

One more detail in this story about my mom: Many years ago, I was able to relate this story to some of my brothers, sister, uncle, aunts, and others at my mom's rest home residence. It was an afternoon "coffee and cookies" session. Mom was there. I had never told the story with her present. Her reaction? "You know, I don't remember that." She performed so many acts of kindness and fed so many people that she could not remember that hot day in 1949. (Butch)

I remember my mom singing this chorus:

Let the beauty of Jesus be seen in me—
All His wonderful passion and purity!
O Thou Spirit divine, all my nature refine,
Till the beauty of Jesus be seen in me.
Osborne

Talk about *incarnational living*!

Epilogue 2

The Balanced Christian Life

I have been inspired by the writings of Charles Caldwell Ryrie.

Perhaps the most spiritually balanced approach to the Christian life is the following:

I. Dedication

1. "Therefore, I urge you brothers, in view of God's mercy, to offer your bodies as living sacrifices holy and pleasing to God—this is your spiritual act of worship. Do not conform to this world, any longer but be transformed by the renewing or your mind. Then you will be able to test and approve what God's will is—His good, pleasing and perfect will." (Romans 12:1–2)
2. Sanctification: separation to the service of God

II. Discipline

1. "If you through the Spirit do mortify the deeds of the body, you shall live." (Romans 8:13)
2. Note: those who have already crucified the flesh (Galatians 5:24) still need to put to death the deeds of the body (tense if present while "crucified" is a past—completed event).
3. The word "You" is the active voice. *We* do it.
4. Death always means separation, never extinction. Ryrie states, "Death to self is not extinction of the self-life but separation from its power. So putting to death the deeds of the body does not mean that those deeds will no longer be a part of our *existence*, but it can mean that they need not be any longer part of our *experience*."

III. Dependence

1. "This I say then, walk in the Spirit, and you shall not fulfill the lust of the flesh" (Galatians 5:16). Constant dependence on the power of the indwelling Spirit of God is essential to the spiritual growth and victory.
2. Thus self-discipline and Spirit-dependence can and must be practiced at the same time in a balanced spiritual life.

IV. Development

1. But if we walk in the light, as He is in the light, we have fellowship one with another, and the blood of Jesus Christ His Son cleanseth us from sin (1 John 1:7). (Keeps on cleansing us.)
2. The cleansing that is referred to in this verse is the cleansing we receive *as* we walk in the light. This is the normal development of the Christian Life. Walking in the light brings additional light and cleansing of those previously darkened areas. Walking (by us), enlightening (by the Word), cleans-

ing (by the blood)—this is the repeating cycle of Christian development.

This is the road of maturing spiritual life—a *dedicated* life that is *disciplined*, *dependent*, and *developing*.

"We see unseen things. We conquer by yielding. We find rest under a yoke. We reign by serving. We are made great by becoming small. We are exalted when we are humble. We become wise by being fools for Christ's sake. We are made free by becoming bondservants. We gain strength when we are weak. We triumph through defeat. We find victory by glorying in our infirmities. We live by dying." (Unknown Author)

EPILOGUE 3

Prayer

"Pray to God in the storm—but keep on rowing." (Danish Proverb)

I have been attending prayer meetings since I was about seven years old. I know that I could have repeated many of the same prayers when those faithful men at church would take their turn to pray at our old Wednesday night prayer services. They would usually use the same old phrases, the same old clichés, and utterances that a former pastor used, repeated over and over again, with seemingly little passion and concern. I attended *every* Wednesday night for ten years until I entered college. I loved those men, but they didn't give a model conducive to learning how to pray.

I grew up with prayer. I remember my folks praying. When I was two years old, my brother Kenneth passed away.

The following was written by my brother, Butch.

> In the fall of 1944, a young man by the name of Kenneth Ralph Quam was injured in the head while playing football in Hawley, MN.

Unknown to him and others, he had developed a brain tumor. Painful headaches followed for weeks. In October, he had surgery in Rochester, MN. His father Andrew and his mother Louise accompanied him to the Mayo Clinic. His father's last words to his son before the operation were, "Give your heart to Christ, Kenny," to which his son replied, "All right, Dad." After the surgery, his father left for home to work and to pray with their church. The church was having special meetings with Rev. Abe Voth at the time. Kenny's mother stayed with her son after the surgery. Later, she prayed alone into the night for him. About 4:00 a.m., she finally gave her son over to the Lord, praying, "I give him to you. Let him die; only save his soul." At 7:00 a.m. that morning, Kenny passed away. Three months after a large and sad funeral, a cousin of Kenny had a dream. The dream was later revealed to Kenny's father, Andrew Quam. In the dream the cousin saw Kenny, who told her, "Tell Mom I'm saved."

My brother, Kenneth Quam, in his high
school basketball uniform

The following are lyrics to a song I wrote. It is a prayer from heaven by Kenny. The music is from the opera "The Pearl Fishers" by Georges Bizet.

A few fleeting years
Filled with laughter and tears;
His Mama prayed all night;
His Daddy urged him to the light.
Tell my Mother,
Tell her that I'm saved.
Tell my Father,
Streets up here with gold are paved.
I have been redeemed,
Bought with blood and am now set free.
I am born again;

Some day you will all come join me.
I saw my sinful condition;
I saw Christ, my redemption,
And now I've received my salvation.
So tell my Mother,
Tell her that I'm saved.
Tell my Father,
Streets up here with gold are paved.
I have been redeemed,
Bought with the blood and am now set free.
I am born again;
Some day you will all come join me.

My mother did not fully recover from Kenny's death. I remember going with her to the cemetery outside of Hawley to water the flowers on Kenny's grave. She spent an inordinate amount of time going to the cemetery. In my entire ministry, the worst heartache I have observed is the emotional pain of a mother experiencing the death of a child.

About the year 1964, I joined a group of musicians (fellow band members from Moorhead State University), to greet Doc Severenson at the airport. This was before he became famous on the *Tonight Show with Johnny Carson*. He was coming to Moorhead, MN, to attend the Nels Volgel music clinic. Right there in Hector Airport, Doc Severenson joined us in a jam session. That impressed Doc Severenson. He never forgot it.

Doc Severenson plays scales for two hours a day. Think of it—two hours a day! I once took lessons on the French horn. The book we studied was written by a member of the Chicago Symphony. He said, "If I don't practice for one day, I know it. If I don't practice for two days, my friends know it. If I don't practice for three days, the whole world knows it."

Think of spending two hours a day in prayer! Powerful! When I entered the ministry October of 1972, my first sermon series was based on prayer. I early installed a prayer chain, etc. I was dogmatic in my preaching. I wanted to write a book: *10 Reasons For Praying*.

Now, after about forty years, I want to write a book entitled *10 Questions About Prayer*. I have learned much about prayer. I treasure it. But I am still learning.

When my stroke happened, I suddenly forgot how to pray. I told my brother in halting speech of my plight. He said, "Don't worry, the Lord knows all about it." I forgot the missionaries' names, fellow pastors, all kinds of names that I would bring to the Lord in prayer. Nothing came to mind. During the twelve days of hospitalization and on to the apartment dwelling, I slowly remembered prayer. It was like being reborn in my prayer life. I remembered key verses on prayer, how to pray, principles of prayer in a new way. I would guess that about four-fifths of my prayers consisted of God speaking to me. During the long hours, I would listen to God speaking through the Scriptures. I could not articulate how to talk with Him. But He continued to speak, through Scripture, to me. The following are principles and thoughts on prayer:

Prayer Reveals Our Spiritual Condition

John Wesley said that "our prayer life is our spiritual barometer. Tell me what your private prayer life is like, and I will tell you what your spiritual life is like."

Prayer Is Talking with God

At best, prayer is a dialogue, not a monologue where you present Him with a shopping list. Be free to express how you feel.

No Time? Pray More

I found that prayer is the most time-saving thing you can do. Learn to work smarter—not harder.

God's Word Teaches Us to Pray

Spend time praying and studying God's Word—a little more each day. We learn to pray when we study the scriptures.

From an unknown source comes this tribute to scripture:

> "These are words written by kings, by emperors, by princes, by poets, by sages, by philosophers, by fisherman, by statesmen, by men learned in the wisdom of Egypt, educated in the schools of Babylon, and trained at the feet of rabbis in Jerusalem. It was written by men in exile, in the desert, in shepherd's tents, in green pastures, and beside still waters. Among its authors we find a tax-gatherer, a herdsman, and a gatherer of Sycamore fruit. We find poor men, rich men, statesmen, preachers, captains, legislators, judges, and exiles. The Bible is a library full of history, genealogy, ethnology, law, ethics, prophecy, poetry, eloquence, medicine, sanitary science, political economy, and the perfect rules for personal and social life. And behind every word is the divine author, God Himself."

Study the Prayers in the Bible

Grow in your prayer life by studying the prayers of the Bible such as those of Abraham, Daniel, Nehemiah, the disciples' prayer in Matthew 6, the Lord's Prayer in John 17, and the prayers of Paul and others.

Keep Track of Your Prayers

Compile a prayer list where you can keep track of your prayer requests, answers to prayer and articles on prayer.

God Cares about You

Think of it. *God has always been.* He created the multitude of universes and billions and billions of stars, yet He is interested in your personal life.

Psalm 139:1–4 says, *"O LORD, You have, searched me and You know me. You know when I sit down and when I rise; You perceive my thoughts from afar. You discern my going out and my lying down; You are familiar with all my ways. Before a word is on my tongue You know it completely . . ."* and Psalm 40:1–3 says: *"I waited patiently for the LORD; He heard my cry. He lifted me out of the slimy pit, out of the mud and mire; He set my feet on a rock and gave me a firm place to stand. He put a new song in my mouth, a hymn of praise to our God . . ."*

Leonard Ravenhill said the following:

Prayer is profoundly simple and simply profound. Prayer is the simplest form of speech that infant lips can try, and yet so sublime that it outranges all speech and exhausts man's vocabulary. A Niagara of burning words does not mean that God is either impressed or moved. One of the most profound of Old Testament intercessors had no language—"Her lips moved, but her voice was not heard."

This last statement is from 1 Samuel 1:13 and refers to Hannah as she poured out her heart to God. She was not a "great linguist."
Romans 8:26 states, "But the Spirit Himself makes intercessions for us with groaning which cannot be uttered" (NKJV).

God is the Creator and Sustainer of the entire universe. God is almighty and all powerful. God comes down from His heaven to dwell in our hearts when we humbly ask Him.

George MacDonald offered this rationale for prayer:

What if God knows prayer to be the thing we need first and most? What if the main object of prayer is a supplying of our great, our endless need of Himself? Communion with God is the one need of the soul beyond all other need. Prayer is the beginning of that communion, of talking with God, a coming-to-one with Him, which is the sole end of prayer, yea, of existence itself. God wants us for Himself. He desires communion with us. His purpose in prayer is not to make us sit up and beg. He wants us to know Him. Prayer is His method to accomplish that.

If your day is hemmed with prayer, it is less likely to become unraveled.
Anonymous

During my stroke recovery, I feel as though I am being reborn in my prayer life. All the concepts I have learned about prayer are now turning into reality. God has ordained prayer. It is His vehicle in learning about Him. My only regret is time wasted in doing other things instead of seeking His face—in prayer.

This treatise has taught about humor--it's anatomy, it's science, it's necessity, it's essence and it's honored place in my life and yours. I believe humor is a gift from God, who gives good gifts to His children. Proverbs 17:22 states: "A cheerful heart is good medicine, but a crushed spirit dries up the bones."

Imagining life today without great humor, comics to entertain us, movies and more makes life look bleak--like a grey, rainy day. Yet, each of us could certainly enjoy life without humor: we would find a way to cope.

What about the subject that is infinitely more important than humor, indeed, more important than anything on this Earth? That is the subject of *eternity.*

According to the Bible, each and everyone of us is faced with a choice: will we *accept* the truths about the Gospel of Christ or will we *reject* them?

The Gospel teaches that Jesus Christ, wholly God and wholly man, perfect in every way, died on a cross to take away the sin of the world, that He was buried and that He rose again, according to the Scriptures. (See 1 Corinthians 15:1-4) He did this to rescue each man, woman and child from an eternity separated from God.

It has been said that a person can live without a lot of things, but one cannot live without *hope*.

I present to you that the only true hope for life and eternity spent in the presence of God is a relationship with the Lord Jesus Christ by grace and through faith.

Where you will spend eternity is, indeed, *No Laughing Matter*.

CPSIA information can be obtained
at www.ICGtesting.com
Printed in the USA
BVHW092249221220
595993BV00004B/52